At Issue

Is Selling Body Parts Ethical?

Other Books in the At Issue Series:

At Issue

Is Selling Body Parts Ethical?

Christine Watkins, Book Editor

GREENHAVEN PRESS
A part of Gale, Cengage Learning

GALE
CENGAGE Learning·

Detroit • New York • San Francisco • New Haven, Conn • Waterville, Maine • London

Elizabeth Des Chenes, *Director, Publishing Solutions*

For more information, contact:
Greenhaven Press
27500 Drake Rd.
Farmington Hills, MI 48331-3535
Or you can visit our Internet site at gale.cengage.com

For product information and technology assistance, contact us at

Gale Customer Support, 1-800-877-4253
For permission to use material from this text or product, submit all requests online at www.cengage.com/permissions

Further permissions questions can be emailed to permissionrequest@cengage.com

Articles in Greenhaven Press anthologies are often edited for length to meet page requirements. In addition, original titles of these works are changed to clearly present the main thesis and to explicitly indicate the author's opinion. Every effort is made to ensure that Greenhaven Press accurately reflects the original intent of the authors. Every effort has been made to trace the owners of copyrighted material.

Cover image © Images.com/Corbis.

LIBRARY OF CONGRESS CATALOGING-IN-PUBLICATION DATA

Is selling body parts ethical? / Christine Watkins, book editor.
    p. cm. -- (At issue)
    Includes bibliographical references and index.
    ISBN 978-0-7377-6189-4 (hardcover) -- ISBN 978-0-7377-6190-0 (pbk.)
    1. Donation of organs, tissues, etc.--Moral and ethical aspects I. Watkins, Christine, 1951-
    RD129.5.I87 2012
    174.2'97954--dc23
                                                        2012015805

Printed in the United States of America
   1 2 3 4 5   16 15 14 13 12

FD270

Contents

Introduction

When Genae Girard was thirty-six years old, she was diagnosed with breast cancer. Because she was relatively young to receive such a diagnosis, her doctor suspected she may have inherited the genes that predispose women to breast and ovarian cancer. Girard was tested through a BRAC Analysis, a blood test in which lab technicians examine two genes—BRCA1 and BRCA2—looking for irregularities. If irregularities in the genes are found, the risk of getting breast cancer is five times more likely and of ovarian cancer as much as forty times more likely than for women with no gene irregularities. Girard tested positive for the mutated genes, and her doctor recommended that she have a double mastectomy and both ovaries removed. Wanting to be sure that the test was accurate, Girard requested a second opinion. "I mean I'm still in my thirties, and this is going to change my life whether or not I ever want to have children," she told CBS News correspondent Morley Safer in 2010. But Girard's doctor informed her it would be impossible to get a second opinion because the molecular diagnostic company that did the original test, Myriad Genetics, owns the exclusive rights to her BRCA1 and BRCA2 genes. "They own the genes, lock stock and barrel. They patented them and no one else can legally test for them, or look at them, or even develop potential therapies that are based on them without Myriad's consent," wrote CBS News in the 2010 article "Should Firms Be Able to Own Your Genes?"

Lisbeth Ceriani came up against the same obstacle. After being diagnosed with breast cancer, Ceriani wanted the genetic test to determine if she was also at risk for ovarian cancer and whether her daughter might have inherited the cancer genes. But Ceriani could not afford the $3,200 that Myriad Genetics charges for the test and had nowhere else to turn. To Ceriani, it did not make sense that a company could "own" the genes inside her body. Anthony Romeri, executive director of the American Civil Liberties Union (ACLU) agreed with her and said in a May 2009 press statement, "Knowledge about our own bodies and the ability to make decisions about our health care are some of our most personal and fundamental rights. The government should not be granting private entities control over something as personal and basic to who we are as our genes." After all, patents are awarded for inventions, and genes are not invented. Furthermore, the federal patent statute maintains that products of nature and laws of nature are not patentable. As Lori Andrews, a professor at Chicago-Kent College of Law, told CBS News correspondent Morley Safer in 2010, "You're right about what the patent law was intended to do, which was to reward inventors who brought something new in the world. But the patent on human genes, it's as if the first surgeon who took a kidney out of your body then patented the kidney." In fact, many people might not be aware that the US Patent and Trademark Office (USPTO) has granted over three thousand patents on human genes, including those associated with Alzheimer's disease, muscular dystrophy, polycystic kidney disease, colon cancer, and asthma. A 2005 study published in the journal *Science* estimated 20 percent of all human genes are patented, of which 63 percent are owned by private firms.

The situation could soon change, however, for cancer patients like Genae Girard and Lisbeth Ceriani. They have joined the ACLU, the Public Patent Foundation of the Benjamin Cardozo School of Law at Yeshiva University in New York, four scientific organizations representing more than 150,000 researchers and laboratory professionals, the women's organizations Breast Cancer Action and Our Bodies Ourselves, and several individual researchers and genetic counselors in a lawsuit against the USPTO, Myriad Genetics, and the University of Utah Research Foundation. The lawsuit, *Association for Molecular Pathology, et al. v. U.S. Patent and Trademark Office, et al.* has made its way through the courts and now hopes the US Supreme Court will invalidate the patents for human genes associated with hereditary breast and ovarian cancer. "We are asking the Court to rule that patent law cannot impede the rights of scientists and doctors to conduct their research and exchange ideas freely," said Chris Hansen, staff attorney with the ACLU Speech Privacy and Technology Project. "Something as natural as human DNA cannot be owned by a particular company."

In response, defenders of gene patents maintain that the process of isolating the DNA from the body and purifying the genes transforms them into entirely different things, which makes them patentable. They further claim that without the economic reward that patents provide, few biotechnology companies would undertake the huge financial investments necessary to conduct research—research that often takes years to produce scientific breakthroughs. As Marcy Darnovsky and Jesse Reynolds wrote in their 2009 *The American Interest* article "The Battle to Patent Your Genes," defenders of gene patents argue that "without patent protection, biotech companies would be unable to fund the research and development of new drugs and treatment—processes that may be privately profitable but also publicly beneficial. They claim, in short, that without patents, there will be no cures." And John Chalfee of the American Enterprise Institute maintains that "patients are the beneficiaries" of gene patents.

The debate about patenting human genes brings to light the concept of "owning" body parts and the implication that human bodies can be sources of material to be exploited for profit. The authors in *At Issue: Is Selling Body Parts Ethical?* discuss other concerns regarding buying and selling parts of the human body.

1

The Sale of Human Organs Should Be Allowed

Jennifer Monti

Jennifer Monti has a medical and a master's degree in public health. Her research work has been published in academic journals, and her other writings have received recognition from the New York Times *and the American Association of Medical Colleges.*

Over 100,000 Americans have kidney or liver disease and need an organ transplant to survive. Nevertheless, the fact is that there are not enough donated organs to meet the high demand. Currently, compensating organ donors is prohibited by the National Organ Transplant Act of 1984 (NOTA), which has led desperate people on the transplant waiting list to turn to a thriving black market in order to purchase the necessary organ. The US Congress needs to repeal the section of NOTA entitled "Prohibition of Organ Purchases" and create a regulated market for the buying and selling of human organs. Such a market would increase the number of donated organs and save countless lives, thus benefitting society.

Demand for kidneys exceeds the current supply of deceased donor organs and altruistic donors. Approximately 73,000 people sit on the waiting list for a kidney—18 of them will die by tomorrow and 6,000 more patients join the list every year. By 2010, over 100,000 Americans will wait for a kidney donation. A kidney transplant in the United States generally requires a five-year wait.

Waiting patients with liver failure have increasingly elevated levels of toxins in their blood. They will become confused, and bleed because their liver fails to make clotting proteins. Patients suffering from kidney failure can languish on dialysis—which is only partially effective at removing toxins from the body—and may die because of complications from it—including low blood pressure, cramps, nausea, vomiting, bleeding, and infection.

Transplant patients enjoy better medical outcomes than dialysis patients. After five years, 65 percent of patients still on dialysis have died, compared with 25 percent of transplant patients. Organs fail more quickly in patients who wait three years for a transplant versus patients who receive one immediately. Furthermore, medical evidence demonstrates that organs from live donors perform better than deceased donor tissue. Live organ donations produce better results, including fewer complications and higher life expectancies, than cadaveric donations or hemodialysis.

The wait for a liver is roughly 430 days. Demand is less because liver disease is less common and there is no treatment analogous to dialysis to support liver failure patients, so death comes more quickly to those in end-stage liver disease.

Legislation and the Rise of Illegal Organ Markets

Ethical and legal debates over paying live organ donors have raged as long as transplantation has existed. In the United States, the National Organ Transplant Act [NOTA] states:

> It shall be unlawful for any person to knowingly acquire, receive, or otherwise transfer any human organ for valuable consideration for use in human transplantation if the trans-

fer affects interstate commerce...any person who violates...shall be fined not more than $50,000 or imprisoned not more than 5 years, or both.

Thus, the organ donation system in the United States relies on organs being donated by family members or other altruistic individuals. If no live match emerges, organ procurement systems rely on cadaveric donations in the hopes that a random match can be found for the needy patient. Both of these non-remunerative methods could remain as options in a system that allowed for regulated payment to live organ donors.

The presence of NOTA in the United States, and similar legislation in other developed countries, has not prevented the development of a thriving black market for procurement of organs from live donors. In early 2008, Indian police, in an incursion into Nepal, arrested a physician in Chitwan, 100 miles south of Kathmandu, who had been buying kidneys from poor locals and transplanting them to wealthy Indians and Westerners. Little to no informed consent process accompanies these procedures, and there are reports of "donors" never receiving payment for their organs. Reports on black market surgeries detail operations taking place in outdated, dangerous facilities. Similar stories have been heard in villages near Chennai, India, and in refugee camps in Tamil Nadu [India]. A transparent market could address these gross violations of medical ethics and safety controls. . . .

Permitting and regulating organ sales leads to more humane conditions than outlawing sales.

The moralistic hubris in blocking the creation of a transparent market for live organ donation rests on the belief that life is invaluable, so to place a price tag on an organ, a slice of life, somehow cheapens its individual worth. As University of Chicago law professor Richard Epstein noted in *The Wall*

Street Journal in 2006: "Only a bioethicist would prefer a world in which we have 1,000 altruists per annum and over 6,500 excess deaths over one in which we have no altruists and no excess deaths." The dissonance between such ethical self-righteousness and the reality on the ground comes into even sharper relief when one considers that prohibiting payment for organs sustains an international organ trafficking black market. Observations by medical personnel and academic study groups, as well as data arising from black market transactions and the one legal market, suggest that permitting and regulating organ sales leads to more humane conditions than outlawing sales. . . .

An Argument for Direct Payment to Donors

The only country to have implemented a legal direct payment system for organs from live donors is Iran. Dialysis and Transplant Patient Association (DATPA)—a free-standing nonprofit organization similar to the National Kidney Foundation in the U.S.—administers the market for live organ donation. Donors receive $1,200 and one year of health care from the government, along with a payment from the organ recipient, generally ranging from $2,300 to $4,500. If the organ recipient does not have funds to offer, a charitable organization will provide such remuneration to the donor. The combination of charitable and governmental payments ensures that poor recipients are treated as well as wealthy ones. Financial exchanges take place above board, in terms that include government payment and rewards, in clean, modern operating rooms. There is no waiting list for a kidney in Iran.

The historical development of the live organ donation program—known as a "white" market—in Iran sheds light on the financial consequences of America's decision to forgo such a model. End-stage renal disease (ESRD) was untreatable until the development of widely available dialysis in the 1970s. Public enthusiasm for this scientific advance was extremely high, and Congress extended an invitation to its inventors to demonstrate the product in Washington, D.C. In 1971, National Association of Public Hospitals Vice President Shep Glazer, affected by kidney failure, testified before Congress while receiving dialysis. Not long after, dialysis became a fully funded Medicare benefit, regardless of patient age. In 2005, Medicare paid for dialysis for 341,000 Americans. This will increase to 400,000 patients by 2010, and to 525,000 to 700,000 patients by 2020. Dialysis treatment for ESRD patients cost Medicare $21 billion in 2005. This total represents 6.5 percent of the Medicare budget being spent on 0.8 percent of beneficiaries.

Individuals without family or without a family match have better access to life-saving transplants.

In contrast, dialysis became widely available around the time Iran was emerging from the Iran-Iraq war, and there were insufficient resources to justify use of public funds for such expensive treatment. Patients were initially reimbursed to go abroad and get a transplant, until the live organ donation system came into existence in 1988. Since then, approximately 1,400 Iranians each year have donated kidneys. Kidneys from living unrelated donors constitute 80 percent of the supply of kidneys in Iran. Unfortunately, many donors from lower socioeconomic strata believe that selling a kidney will solve their financial problems. While such perceptions are undesirable, the presence of a regulated market has removed any illegal market from Iran, while extinguishing organ broker price mark-ups or transplants in dirty facilities with marginally skilled surgeons. Individuals without family or without a family match have better access to life-saving transplants.

Economists at the University of Chicago have estimated a kidney to be worth $15,200. These estimates were compared to the average price agreed upon among 305 sellers in India in

2005 ($1,177). This estimate corroborates very well with the underground kidney market in India. When adjusted for standards of living, the price paid in India for a kidney equals $17,000. Similar modeling estimates a liver donation to be worth $37,600 to the donor. Current costs of procuring an organ for transplant in the United States are over $50,000. These estimates demonstrate that the cost of transplants would effectively go down in a well-supplied market system. Legislative action to legalize direct payment for organ donation would result in substantial cost savings to a government spending exorbitantly for dialysis treatments. Cost savings occurs if a recipient lives free of dialysis for more than 1.5 years; 95 percent of organ recipients would fall into this category.

In the United States, a direct payment system for live organ donation could be regulated and managed by the United Network for Organ Sharing (UNOS), in a similar manner to the non-profit organization established in Iran. UNOS currently manages the waiting list for potential organ recipients. It has over 20 years of experience in managing the cadaveric donor pool and could easily extend its jurisdiction to include donation by living donors. Even if a system of payment for organ donations were instituted in the United States, UNOS could continue to allocate organs to recipients on the basis of medical, not social or economic, criteria, in line with NOTA guidelines.

An Argument for Indirect Payment to Donors

Advocates of an incentivized organ donation program have seized on the vague term "valuable consideration" in NOTA in an effort to clarify and expand what states and other institutions can offer to potential donors without being in conflict with federal law. In 2007, Wisconsin enacted a law that gives living donors a tax deduction of up to $10,000 for medical costs, travel, and lost wages. Recent changes to federal law suggest a growing recognition among policy makers of the need for incentivization. In 2004, the Organ Donation and Recovery Improvement Act authorized the federal government to reimburse live-organ donors for costs incurred donating an organ. Policy makers claim that these programs do not pay people directly for donating an organ, but, rather, "keep them from losing money" (which is akin to companies offering benefits in lieu of pay raises).

In 2008, Sen. Arlen Specter (R-Penn.) tried to get support for a proposed Organ Donor Clarification Act, which would remove any legal concern states have expressed that their programs may run afoul of NOTA. This bill would allow non-cash incentives for organ donation, including tax breaks, health insurance, or funeral benefits. While the bill keeps the ban on organ *sales* intact, barring the explicit commercialization of organs, it does effectively allow organs to become commodities of value.

While indirect payments for donation are a promising step, a better proposal to increase the number of organ donors would be for Congress to repeal Section 301 of the National Organ Transplant Act. Section 301, entitled "Prohibition of Organ Purchases," imposes criminal penalties of up to $50,000 and five years in prison on any person who "knowingly acquire[s], receive[s], or otherwise transfer[s] any human organ for valuable consideration for use in human transplantation, if the transfer affects interstate commerce." This ought to be replaced with legislation that designates a nonprofit organization like UNOS as a clearinghouse for organ brokerage arrangements. . . .

Answering the Critics

Market critics fret that offering payment will be coercive to the poor, who need the money the most. While it may be true that poorer people would be more likely to donate an organ in exchange for payment, it is also likely that poorer people are more likely to take any sort of job for payment. The poor are also more likely to take jobs that entail a higher risk of death, like coal mining or fishing—yet governments allow them to participate in these activities for money despite the higher risk. Is it coercive to offer a poor person any sort of job?

This "exploitation" criticism is paternalistically condescending. Is a poor individual unable to properly judge the risks and benefits of donating an organ under such a system? The organization responsible for regulating this market would administer informed consent procedures to ensure that every donor is fully informed, willing, and able to make such a decision.

Parts of the living body are bought and sold every day by consenting American adults.

Critics of payment for live organ donation go so far as to compare such transactions to prostitution. This analogy muddles the distance between the physical and emotional investments inherent in prostitution and the mundane relationship that most people have with a kidney or a liver lobe. In the United States, oocytes and sperm can be freely sold to assist people with infertility, and those payments seem, on their face, more emotionally invested than kidney or liver donation.

Perhaps it is the critics' concern that organs, rather than cells or tissues, are so valuable that any amount of money would not be enough. This begs the question: Enough money for whom?

In addition to egg and sperm cells, other parts of the living body are bought and sold every day by consenting American adults. Tens of thousands of Americans sell their blood plasma to companies that subsequently create intravenous immune globulin (IVIG) to treat myriad diseases from Kawasaki disease in children to autoimmune myopathies in adults.

Plasma donors earn $40 per week for their trouble. Demand is expected to increase as the value of IVIG continues to be demonstrated in entreating a variety of diseases.

Selling plasma to a private firm is legal, but selling whole blood is not. However, blood donation organizations are able to sell donor blood on the open market and use the funds to support other businesses. In 1989, nearly two-thirds of the Red Cross's $2.1 billion in revenue came from the sale of blood and plasma products collected in donations. Demand for plasma has skyrocketed since then, and the Red Cross relies on these sales to fund its operations. Why should the Red Cross make a profit from an individual's donation, but the individual is barred from doing so?

Consider the flow of resources and rewards in organ transactions. The organ recipient will gain in quality of life and increased income from a greater ability to work. Hospitals and medical professionals also benefit. For hospitals, transplant is often a low-volume, high margin business for which there is competition. Hospitals charge $400,000 to $500,000 for a liver transplant. The University of Pittsburgh's transplant program produced $130 million of revenue in its latest fiscal year. Concerns that payment stains the dignity of the donor ring hollow when everyone involved in the process enjoys material gain or prestige—except the donor. . . .

The debate over payment for live organ donation comes into sharpest focus when applied to real people in the medical office. By the time the sun sets today, 18 people will have died waiting for a kidney transplant that never arrived. Several people with liver disease will turn a darker shade of yellow as bilirubin piles up in the blood. Medical science is ready and waiting to save these people's lives, but policy remains a roadblock. The development of a regulated market for payment to live organ donors will drastically reduce the waiting lists for organ transplants in the United States. How much is that worth? The smart money is on priceless.

2

The Sale of Human Organs Is Unethical

Debra Budiani-Saberi and Deborah M. Golden

Debra Budiani-Saberi is the founder and executive director of the Coalition for Organ-Failure Solutions (COFS), an international nonprofit health and human rights organization with a mission to combat exploitative forms of organ donation. Deborah M. Golden is a member of the board of directors of COFS and is also a staff attorney at the Washington Lawyers' Committee for Civil Rights and Urban Affairs.

Organ transplants have become a life-saving therapy for thousands of people, and the demand for organs from patients with organ failure far exceeds the supply. Because of the great demand, there is a growing appeal to create a system that compensates organ donors. Other countries have created such organ markets with problematic results, such as exploitation of the poor and negative health consequences. Other and more ethical methods to increase the supply of donated organs can be implemented without debasing body parts into commodities or exploiting impoverished people.

Yuri, a 29-year-old Egyptian man residing in the outskirts of Cairo, worked an average of 12 hours a day on a bus calling out destinations at bus stops and collecting passengers' fees. When his dire living conditions worsened, it led him to desperation. "Many circumstances led me to this—my mother needed an intestinal surgery and my two sisters needed to marry. I no longer had a place to live and began to sleep on the streets." Yuri met a man at a bus stop who had sold his own kidney and found out how he could do this himself to help solve his family's problems.

The laboratory made a match and Yuri met Sherif, a 60-year-old auto service center owner who needed a kidney and would pay 2,200 USD [US dollars] to Yuri for his "donation." Yuri experienced pain, nausea and loss of appetite for weeks after his surgery. Several months passed before he could return to work, but even then he felt easily fatigued while standing long hours and had to take time off from work intermittently.

Eighty-one percent of commercial living donors (CLDs) in Egypt spend their "kidney money" within five months after their kidney sale. This was also the case for Yuri. While the money helped finance his mother's surgery and living expenses for his siblings, Yuri's circumstances did not improve and he continued to reside on Cairo's streets. . . .

The History of the National Organ Transplant Act of 1984 (NOTA)

The U.S. Congress passed NOTA in 1984 as the first attempt to regulate the growing practice of organ donation and transplantation in the country. Until the discovery of cyclosporine, an anti-rejection drug, and its FDA [US Food and Drug Administration] approval in the early 1980s, widespread organ transplants between individuals not closely related were not possible. The issue of material incentives rose to national prominence at the time because the first organ market was opening in the United States. Dr. H. Barry Jacobs, a private doctor in Virginia, planned to pay donors their asking price for a kidney, add a few thousand dollars to the price for a profit, and sell the kidneys to recipients or to Medicaid and Medicare programs. At that time, there were no legal prohibitions that would have prevented this doctor from implementing such a scheme.

It is ethically offensive to look at organs and body parts the same way as we look at fenders from automobiles in the junkyard.

Reports of possible payment created a deluge of desperate offers from potential donors with no other hope of financial support. Robert Steinberg offered his kidney for $25,000 to the University of Wisconsin-Madison Hospital and Clinics. He also offered to sell his left eye. He said "Financially, I am in an awful mess. . . I don't want to be on welfare." Bob Reina placed a classified ad to sell his kidney for $12,000. Steve Pollock had mortgaged his business and with no way to get a loan from a bank, took out an ad to sell a kidney for $25,000. David Severn, faced with mounting debts and a house that would not sell in a down market, offered to sell a kidney, eye, or part of any other organ to raise $5,000. Joseph Greco placed a similar ad after he had to sell his refrigerator for money and was keeping his food in an ice chest. He was willing to simply trade his kidney for a job. These reports illuminated the economic desperation that drives people to an organ market. Then, as now, these stories evoked disgust and sadness at the idea that people were driven to such extremes in order to survive.

Public opinion quickly coalesced around the idea of banning such commodification. Dr. Ira Greifer, medical director of the National Kidney Foundation, derided the idea of the poor selling their organs as "supply-side cannibalism." Lawmakers moved to pass NOTA in order to prohibit a market in body parts. Rep. Henry Waxman [Democratic US Representative from California] explained that "it is ethically offensive to look at organs and body parts the same way as we look at fenders from automobiles in the junkyard." Ultimately, lawmakers passed NOTA, section 301 of which prohibits the acquisition, sale or transfer of any human organ for transplantation for "valuable consideration," upon penalty of up to a fine of $50,000 and five years imprisonment.

Proposed Legislation for Financial Benefits to Organ Donors

Demand for organs remains high and unfulfilled. Various transplant professionals, academics, and attorneys in the United States and abroad argue that a regulated market in human organs would reduce the patient waiting list for organs and in turn work to ameliorate the global illicit market and conditions of poverty for organ vendors. In the United States, proponents of a regulated market have gained support from influential think tanks that favor market-based approaches such as the American Enterprise Institute for Public Policy Research and the Cato Institute.

Proposals by market proponents have included financial payouts or non-monetary benefits in exchange, or as a "reward," for an organ. The most commonly mentioned incentive is a tax deduction or a tax credit. Either of these is in essence a government pay-out. Another proposed financial incentive is college tuition credits. Incentives that are not inherently fungible yet still valuable include job benefits, the shortening of prison sentences, or the commutation of a death sentence to one of life in prison.

Senator [Arlen] Specter [Democrat from Pennsylvania] has circulated at least five drafts of a proposed bill, now entitled the Organ Trafficking Prohibition Act of 2009 (OTPA). The OTPA is an undertaking by proponents of material incentives to amend NOTA such that a government entity would be permitted to provide compensation for an organ donation. The most recent version available as of this writing [June 2009] states:

> The Federal and State constitutions empower the governments to provide a benefit to individuals who donated the gift of life to fellow citizens. The sovereign's provision of a gratuitous benefit to organ donors is not commercial in nature and does not constitute a commercial sales transaction. . . .

The OTPA proceeds to list potential government benefits that could be granted to organ donors in the U.S. including: medals, those benefits provided to veterans, tax credits and deductions, discounts or waivers of drivers' license fees, life insurance, disability and survivor benefits, a modest donation to a donor's chosen charity, preference on the transplant waiting list, and tax credits for employers who pay lost wages. To implement the proposed policy change, the bill would exempt all "actions taken by the Government of the United States or any state, territory, tribe, or local government to the United States to encourage organ donation" from NOTA's prohibition on organ trafficking, selling, and purchasing.

Markets not only exploit donors, but also fail to meet the demand for organs, and may even harm organ recipients.

To be clear, this bill is not meant simply to allow small tokens of appreciation to be provided by the government. Rather, the OTPA aims to legalize government compensation of substantial financial benefits otherwise out of reach for most Americans, especially in financially perilous times. Under this proposed bill, any imaginable compensation provided by any level of government would be legal—there are no proposed limits. The government could conceivably compensate organ donors with anything ranging from citizenship, to commutation of penal sentences, to financial benefits. . . .

Faults of Material Incentives for Organ Donation

A system based on financial or material incentives for donation is inherently flawed. This premise is supported by evidence that demonstrates that organ markets are universally problematic—both in the world's only regulated market in Iran as well as in the black and grey markets that exist in many other countries. Markets not only exploit donors, but also fail to meet the demand for organs, and may even harm organ recipients.

First, material incentives necessarily target the poor by providing inducements for their "donation." A material payment for an organ most appeals to those individuals with insufficient employment, health care, housing or education. It may even be coercive in a situation where a compensated organ donation is the only alternative for a destitute individual or family. This was the case in the United States before NOTA was enacted, with desperate people seeing organ-selling as their only alternative.

It would not be possible to completely regulate a market in organs domestically.

Second, material incentives would induce less-than-healthy donors to come forward and thus do not secure the best health outcomes for either recipients or donors. Payments for organ donations lure potential donors (and their profiting parties) to deny that they may have been exposed to HIV/AIDS, hepatitis, or tuberculosis. While appropriate donor assessment protocols should always be in place for a donor and recipient's well-being, screening diseases with incubation periods, such as HIV, cannot always produce results with certainty. Positive health outcomes must rely on structures of trust that will be hurt with the introduction of material incentives in exchange for organ donation.

Third, such incentives are likely to undermine altruistic living and deceased donation. Individuals will be less likely to request a donation from a family member if there is an alternative. . . .

Finally, it would not be possible to completely regulate a market in organs domestically when, as with other commodities, global prices/rewards would vary. State compensation for organ donation is still unlikely to satisfy demand because patients who opt to shorten their wait-time and can afford to go abroad for an organ will continue to do so. Insomuch as patients might bear a portion of the financial burden for a compensated donation, they would also have reason to go where prices were affordable. The proposals in OTPA would not ameliorate these dynamics that facilitate organ trafficking.

OTPA is not immune to these flaws. The bill would inevitably attract lower-income or vulnerable individuals into organ donation for compensation. It would also fundamentally change the structure of organ donation in America by abandoning our altruistic system and replacing it with a system based on calculated materialism. Insomuch as patients may also bear a cost of obtaining the commodified organ in the OTPA's scheme, they are likely to go where prices and the wait time is most accommodating.

Experts on organ transplants and trafficking recently established the following definition of terms at international meetings on organ trafficking in Istanbul to capture the range of practices involved in the phenomenon. The definitions developed in Istanbul are useful to review here, as they describe the boundaries of markets around the world.

Transplant commercialism is a policy or practice in which an organ is treated as a commodity, including by being bought or sold or used for material gain.

Organ trafficking is the recruitment, transport, transfer, harboring or receipt of living or deceased persons or their organs by means of the threat or use of force or other forms of coercion, of abduction, of fraud, of deception, of the abuse of power or of a position of vulnerability, or of the giving to, or the receiving by, a third party of payments or benefits to achieve the transfer of control over the potential donor, for the purpose of exploitation by the removal of organs for transplantation.

These definitions capture the variety of practices that are based on material incentives and compensation for organ donation that operate globally. These practices include regulated conditions, loosely structured trade, and flagrant abuses of the "donor." Compensated organ donation in other nations also sheds light on the consideration of such a scheme in the United States and the consequences that would result from it.

Consequences of Organ Markets in Foreign Countries

Several countries, including Kuwait and Saudi Arabia, have compensated live donors and families of the deceased as a part of the consent process for procuring organs. These countries have received criticism, however, as such donations have almost unanimously been from non-national laborers of the Indian sub-continent rather than national Kuwaitis and Saudis. Only in Iran has commercial living organ donation been officially regulated by the government. In the Iranian system, government-affiliated groups match organ sellers and buyers, who set their own prices for the deal. As discussed below, this framework has not prevented exploitative measures that take advantage of the poor as organ suppliers. It has also not closed the door on additional off-record payments to donors and fees to recipients.

Apart from these nations in which there are regulatory schemes for commercial living organ donation, unregulated practices have thrived in many parts of the world as a staple source of supplying organs for transplant. Although such practices are technically illegal in Egypt, the institution that issues medical licenses (the Doctors' Syndicate), transplant centers and laboratories openly tolerate and accommodate commercial transplants. Unlicensed transplants in Egypt reflect similar abuses of organ trafficking that operate in other global hot spots including Pakistan and the Philippines.

Poverty, vulnerability and destitution are social determinants for commercial living organ donation that remain consistent throughout the wide variety of contexts of the global trade in organs. Studies on CLDs who donated a kidney in Egypt, India, Iran, Pakistan, and the Philippines indicate that CLDs are poorly educated, unemployed, and uninsured individuals living under the poverty line. Most individual donors resort to a commercial living organ donation to solve a personal financial crisis.

Organs flow as commodities from poor and vulnerable individuals to those who are better off.

Negative health consequences for CLDs have become evident in these studies. CLDs have consistently reported a general deterioration in their health status—78% in Egypt, 86% in India, 60% in Iran, 98% in Pakistan, and 48% in the Philippines. Further follow-up study is required to better understand these findings, but each of these studies indicates that most CLDs felt their health status worsened as a result of kidney donation. The Iranian study included specific inquiries about CLDs' health consequences and desires for health improvement. Half the CLDs would have preferred to lose more than 10 years of their lives and to lose 76–100% of their personal possessions in return for their preoperative condition. . . .

These consequences occurred in countries with distinct contexts, including a regulated market in Iran, tolerated/

facilitated commercialism in Egypt, and thriving illegal organ trafficking in India. Thus, commercial transplants, whether regulated or not, are socially arranged such that organs flow as commodities from poor and vulnerable individuals to those who are better off. OTPA would replicate such features in the United States and allow poor and vulnerable American residents to be induced into selling organs for whatever price or privilege a government entity could offer that would sufficiently appeal to potential living organ donors. . . .

Alternative Avenues to Enhance Organ Donation in the U.S.

Increasing the supply of available organs for transplants does not have to depend upon material incentives. There are alternative opportunities for the United States to foster increased altruistic donation. Proposals to permit material incentives distract from other important avenues for increasing organ donation that have yet to reach their maximum potential. . . .

Advances can also be made to enhance altruistic living donation, particularly by improving living donor care and removing disincentives for organ donations. Protocols to improve donor follow-up care have been refined in the Amsterdam and Vancouver Forums on care of the live kidney and liver, lung, pancreas and intestine donor respectively. These should be adopted by all transplant centers that engage live donors. Support should also be extended to live donors to provide job security, assured donor leave, and health and life insurance for donation-related events. Such provisions would serve to provide donor care and remove obstacles for those who wish to be organ donors. If this support were implemented, more individuals considering altruistic living donorship would confront fewer difficulties in the process and be more inclined to go through with the donation. . . .

As illustrated at the beginning of this paper, Yuri resorted to selling a kidney when his poor living conditions became especially destitute and the reward particularly appealing. Those conditions drove him to the donation and he regretted the decision afterwards. Existing transplant commercialism operates in countries that are, by definition, different from the United States. Although proponents of compensated donation suggest that the experience would be different in the U.S., individuals are similarly likely to resort to a donation when compensation includes rewards such as comprehensive health care for life, health and life insurance, disability and survivor benefits or educational benefits. Like the cash payment to Yuri, these forms of compensation are considered to significantly enhance the life of an individual who cannot afford these basic needs.

The United States must join the international community to rebuild, not compromise, trust in transplants. This is especially important at this moment when markets have failed economic and social needs in global and historical dimensions and altruism has become especially priceless. Guided by the WHO [World Health Organization] resolution on organ transplants and the Istanbul Declaration, transplant practices can advance standards of greater social equality rather than exploit people in poverty. There are many opportunities to advance organ donation in the U.S. without subjecting individuals to experiences such as Yuri's.

3

Organ Gangs Force Poor to Sell Kidneys for Desperate Israelis

Michael Smith, Daryna Krasnolutska, and David Glovin

Michael Smith, Daryna Krasnolutska, and David Glovin are journalists for Bloomberg News.

Throughout the world there is a vast shortage of legally donated human organs that thousands of desperately ill people need for transplants in order to survive. As a result of the shortage, criminals have taken the opportunity to make huge profits by creating a black market in the sale of human organs. Such criminals convince or force impoverished people to sell their kidneys for a minimal amount of money and then collect fifteen or twenty times that amount from needy transplant patients. Governments around the world are investigating and prosecuting many of those involved in organ trafficking, but the organized crime activity will continue to prosper as long as there is a shortage of legally donated organs.

Aliaksei Yafimau shudders at the memory of the burly thug who threatened to kill his relatives. Yafimau, who installs satellite television systems in Babrujsk, Belarus, answered an advertisement in 2010 offering easy money to anyone willing to sell a kidney.

He saw it as a step toward getting out of poverty. Instead, Yafimau, 30, was thrust into a dark journey around the globe that had him, at one point, locked in a hotel room for a month in Quito, Ecuador, waiting for surgeons to cut out an organ. . . .

The man holding Yafimau against his will was Roini Shimshilashvili, a former kickboxer who was an enforcer for an international organ-trafficking ring, according to evidence gathered by police in Kiev. Yafimau says that when he pleaded with Shimshilashvili to let him get out of the deal and go home, the big man sliced the air with Thai-boxing moves and threatened him.

"He said if I didn't go through with it, he would leave me in Ecuador and kill my family," Yafimau says.

Doctors removed Yafimau's left kidney in July 2010 and transplanted it into an Israeli woman, according to the Kiev police investigation. On the plane back to Belarus, on the western border of Russia, Shimshilashvili told Yafimau that if he wanted to live, he shouldn't talk to police.

"I am afraid for my life," says Yafimau, standing outside his mother's Babrujsk apartment building, a nine-story, Soviet-era edifice that's surrounded by weeds and trash. The traffickers paid Yafimau $10,000. He says it wasn't worth the fear that haunts him today.

It's against the law to buy or sell an organ in every country except Iran.

Violence and Coercion

Yafimau is one of the faceless and neglected victims in a sprawling global black market in organs—where brokers use deception, violence and coercion to buy kidneys from impoverished people, mainly in underdeveloped countries, and then sell them to critically ill patients in more-affluent nations.

The middlemen form alliances with doctors in leading hospitals who do these transplants for a fee, no questions asked.

Organ trafficking is on the rise, as desperate people seek transplants in a world that doesn't have enough donors. About 5,000 people sell organs on the black market each year, according to Francis Delmonico, an adviser on transplants to the World Health Organization.

It's against the law to buy or sell an organ in every country except Iran, says Delmonico, who is president-elect of the Montreal-based Transplantation Society, which lobbies governments to crack down on illicit procedures.

Traffickers typically pay $10,000 to a seller for a kidney and collect $150,000 when selling it to a patient.

'Exploit Shortages'

"There have been successes fighting organ trafficking around the world," Delmonico says. "But organ trafficking continues to flourish because criminals exploit shortages of organ donors."

Bloomberg Markets reported in June [2011] that U.S. citizens and others from the Americas suffering from kidney failure were going to Nicaragua and Peru to buy organs in a shadowy trade that injured and killed donors and recipients.

That U.S.-Latin American connection is dwarfed by a network of organ-trafficking organizations whose reach extends from former Soviet Republics such as Azerbaijan, Belarus and Moldova to Brazil, the Philippines, South Africa and beyond, a *Bloomberg Markets* investigation shows. . . .

'Obscene Profit'

Criminals see an opportunity to make big money in the organ trade, where they can sell a kidney for 15 to 20 times what they pay, police throughout Europe say.

"They recognize the obscene profit that can be made in the expanding black market in body parts," says Jonathan Ratel, a Pristina, Kosovo-based prosecutor who has been investigating organ trafficking over the past two years. "It keeps happening because there is so much money in this."

Traffickers typically pay $10,000 to a seller for a kidney and collect $150,000 when selling it to a patient.

Traffickers prey on the most vulnerable people Moldova, the poorest country in Europe, is one of their prime hunting grounds.

Dorin Razlog, a shepherd with an eighth-grade education who lives in Ghincauti, says recruiters for a trafficking ring told him cash for a kidney would lift him out of poverty. After doctors in Istanbul cut out the organ in August 2002, they paid him $7,000—$3,000 less than they'd offered. Of that, $2,500 was in counterfeit bills, he says.

Writhing from Pain

"They told me they would send people to destroy my house and kill my family if I went to the police," Razlog, 30, says. Today, the money is long gone, and he sleeps on a musty mattress inside the rusting hulk of an abandoned Russian van next to a pigsty. At the end of some days, Razlog says, he's writhing from pain in his remaining kidney.

"The only way out is death," he says.

The Ukrainian Interior Ministry broke up the ring that bought Razlog's kidney and arrested its leader—a Ukrainian-born Israeli national—in 2007.

In Mingir, Moldova, the organ black market cost a man his life. Vasile Diminetz, a frail retired farmer, says his son Vladimir grew ill after a broker bought his kidney in Turkey for $2,000 in 1999.

Haunted by Memories

Vladimir died in 2003 at the age of 25, after his remaining kidney failed, according to the Renal Foundation of Moldova, which has documented dozens of cases of organ trafficking.

Vasile, 70, stands outside the stone cottage where he lives alone, haunted by the memories.

"If I only knew, I could have saved my boy," he says. "Maybe I could have done more, and I will regret that until I die."

Prosecutors in nine countries have been conducting criminal probes of organ trafficking involving Israeli patients since 2003. The largest case dates to that year, when the Brazilian Federal Police noticed people from two slums of Recife, a coastal city 2,110 kilometers (1,311 miles) from Sao Paulo, flying to Durban, South Africa.

They returned home in so much pain from incisions across their abdomens that they needed assistance to get off the plane, says Karla Gomes de Matos Maia, the investigator who led the probe.

'Suspect Organ Trafficking'

"Here you had people who didn't fit the profile of tourists going to a strange destination and coming back after having major surgery," Maia says. "We began to suspect organ trafficking."

The Brazilian case is still wending its way through international courts. In November 2010 in Durban, Netcare Ltd. (NTC)—South Africa's largest hospital company—pleaded guilty to violating the Human Tissue Act, which prohibits buying and selling organs.

Netcare paid 7.8 million rand ($848,464) in fines and penalties. It admitted to allowing 92 transplants in which donors from Brazil, Israel and Romania sold kidneys to Israeli patients. Four doctors are awaiting trial on trafficking charges.

In Brazil, 12 people connected to the Netcare case were convicted and jailed, with sentences from 15 months to 11 years.

In Kosovo, Ratel, who has dual citizenship in Canada and Great Britain and was appointed by the European Union to help restore the country's criminal justice system, is overseeing a pivotal organ-trafficking case. It includes participants and victims from Belarus, Moldova, Turkey and four other countries.

Center for Trafficking

The EU has administered the courts in Kosovo since 2008, the year the country the size of Connecticut declared independence from Serbia after a civil war. Ratel, who arrived in March 2010 as part of the European Union Rule of Law Mission in Kosovo, says the country has become a center for organ trafficking.

Ratel built a case against nine doctors, hospital administrators and recruiters on charges of buying and selling kidneys for patients in Georgia, Germany, Israel, Poland and Ukraine, as well as Canada and the United States.

The trial began in October and is expected to continue into 2012. He has sought assistance from investigators in 11 countries in the case.

Ratel says he's stunned by the callousness of the criminals who run the organ rings. Traffickers in Kosovo threatened one kidney seller with death if he testified in court, so the court had the man placed into a witness protection program.

While the illegal organ trade may be run by seasoned criminals, it depends on the complicity of doctors and hospitals.

'Threats of Violence'

"This is organized crime," Ratel says. "There is significant coercion and threats of violence."

Organ traffickers search the world for hospitals willing to perform illicit transplants.

Sometimes, sellers are flown to cities just to wait for procedures, and then traffickers move them to other parts of the globe when they find a recipient and a hospital willing to co-operate.

While the illegal organ trade may be run by seasoned criminals, it depends on the complicity of doctors and hospitals, says Oleg Liashko, a member of Ukraine's parliament.

"I doubt this could happen without the hospital and doctors knowing about it," says Liashko, who has investigated organ trafficking and is calling for more-severe criminal penalties in organ transplant laws. "They either know or look the other way because of the money involved. This is corruption, pure and simple."

Doctors must be held criminally accountable when they perform surgery with an organ that's been sold, Ratel says.

'Willful Blindness'

"Ignorance is not a defense," he says. "That is willful blindness. A doctor involved should know all the relevant facts, including whether the donor is a blood relative or not."

People have two kidneys that filter toxins out of the bloodstream. A patient with failure in both kidneys will die quickly unless he or she is hooked up to a dialysis machine or gets a transplant.

Transplants prolong lives, and patients who receive organs from living donors have better survival rates than those who receive organs from deceased donors.

Of patients who get organs from a living donor, 90 percent survive at least five years; for those receiving an organ from a dead donor, the figure is 82 percent, according to the Washington-based Organ Procurement and Transplantation Network. Legitimate organ donors are usually relatives of the patient. . . .

The Israeli-eastern European organ-trafficking rings have also extended their reach to the U.S. In July 2009, the Justice

Department charged Levy Rosenbaum, an Israeli living in New York, with conspiracy to commit human organ trafficking.

A Federal Bureau of Investigation agent says he caught Rosenbaum, who lives in Brooklyn, New York, offering to sell a kidney for $160,000. Rosenbaum was the first, and so far the only, person arrested for organ trafficking in the U.S. since the activity was outlawed in 1984.

Rosenbaum, 60, pleaded guilty on Oct. 27 to brokering the sale of human kidneys. Free on bail, he could be sentenced to five years in prison. He declined to comment.

Rosenbaum worked with Sammy Shem-Tov in Jerusalem to lure young men and women to sell kidneys, according to Avichai Osuna, who says he was recruited to sell a kidney by both men.

Osuna, an unemployed 27-year-old man in Be'er Sheva, a city in the Negev Desert south of Jerusalem, moonlighted as an apprentice for Shem-Tov, before he became a seller. Shem-Tov paid Osuna 1,500 shekels ($410) a month to use his ability to speak English to arrange illegal organ transplants with foreign hospitals, Osuna says.

'Off My Back'

Shem-Tov, 67, asked Osuna to sell his own kidney in June 2008, says Osuna, a heavyset man who wears an earring in his left ear.

"Just to get him off my back and because I needed a little cash, I said all right," he says.

Soon, Osuna told Shem-Tov that he had changed his mind, concerned about the dangers of giving up an organ, according to Shem-Tov's indictment in Jerusalem District Court.

Late one evening, Shem-Tov called Osuna to a meeting in Be'er Sheva. Next to him were two men Shem-Tov described as mafia enforcers, the indictment says. Shem-Tov told Osuna that if he didn't sell a kidney, he'd be in debt to the two men and the mafia group, the indictment says.

"He said, 'You don't want to back out now,'" Osuna says. "I felt trapped."

Constantly Watched

Shem-Tov flew him from Tel Aviv to New York on July 31, 2008, because the trafficker thought he could arrange a transplant in New York, according to Shem-Tov's indictment. Rosenbaum met Osuna at the gate and took his mobile phone and passport.

He had Osuna and other prospective organ sellers housed and constantly watched by a minder in a house near Brooklyn's Prospect Park.

Rosenbaum kept Osuna waiting for six months, Osuna says. While in New York, Rosenbaum brought Osuna to Mount Sinai Medical Center for a blood test, Osuna says. Sander Florman, director of Mount Sinai's Recanati/Miller Transplantation Institute, says the hospital does all it can to avoid illicit procedures.

"We make them jump through incredible hoops," he says. "We have all the rules. People find ways around them."

Threats of Retaliation

The transplant recipient backed out, and Osuna says Rosenbaum sent him back to Israel. A year later, Shem-Tov flew Osuna from Israel to Manila. Osuna tried again to cancel the deal, and his minders threatened him with mafia retaliation, the indictment says.

He says he felt trapped, and a few days later was taken to Cardinal Santos Medical Center. Surgeons removed his left kidney on Oct. 21, 2009, the indictment says.

Four days later, Osuna was on a flight back to Israel, and the recipient, a Tel Aviv man, paid him 94,000 shekels

($26,000). Osuna says he couldn't recover in peace, for fear of what would happen when he got home.

"When I look in the mirror and see that scar, it's a daily reminder of what I went through," he says. "I feel this raw grievance inside."

Cardinal Santos Ethics Committee Chairman Juanito Billote says the hospital can't comment on specific cases to protect patient privacy. The hospital scrutinizes every transplant to ensure it complies with all laws, he says.

As long as there's a worldwide shortage of legal donors for life-saving transplants, the exploitation of the poor will only grow.

'We Make Sure'

"In doing any foreign-to-foreign transplant, we make sure that the rules are adequately addressed," he says.

The laws and rules designed to prevent the trafficking in organs aren't working. While prosecutors in places such as Israel, Brazil, Kosovo and Ukraine have successfully crippled some of the organ-trading gangs, they're fighting powerful economic forces.

As long as there's a worldwide shortage of legal donors for life-saving transplants, the exploitation of the poor will only grow, Kosovo-based prosecutor Ratel says.

"There's burgeoning organized-crime activity in trafficking of human organs," he says. "It will take serious efforts by governments and hospitals to stop it."

Governments around the world need to cooperate to enforce existing laws on illicit procedures, Harvard's Delmonico says. Nations have to ensure they have systems making it safe and easy for people to donate voluntarily, he says. Unless that happens, the traffickers will continue to cultivate a growing legion of impoverished organ sellers who can end up with a quick infusion of cash—and a lifetime of humiliation, pain and illness.

4

A Legal Transparent Organ-Selling Market Would Help Prevent Trafficking

Scott Carney

Scott Carney, an award-winning journalist, is a contributing editor at Wired *magazine and has written stories on a variety of medical, technological, and ethical issues. Carney is also the author of the book* The Red Market: On the Trail of the World's Organ Brokers, Bone Thieves, Blood Farmers, and Child Traffickers.

Although troublesome to accept, it is a fact that body parts are precious commodities and are bought and sold worldwide on what can be called a "red market." Under optimum circumstances, such a market would not exist because enough altruistic donors would give away their organs to keep up with the demand. The reality is, however, that there are not enough donors, and a dire shortage of human organs for transplants exists in the world today. To help prevent criminal red market activity and exploitation of the poor, a regulated and transparent system needs to be set up so that organ donors will be paid and treated with respect, and the shortage of organs can begin to be alleviated.

It doesn't matter what our moral position is on the subject, bodies are unquestionably commodities. And yet they are uncomfortable ones. As a product, bodies aren't assembled new in factories filled with sterile suited workers; rather they are harvested like used cars at scrap markets. Before you can write a check and pick up human tissue, someone needs to transform it from a tiny piece of humanity into something with a market value. Unlike scrap, the price of a human body isn't measured only in dollars. It is measured in blood, and in the ineffable value of lives both saved and lost. When we buy a body part, we take on the liabilities for where it came from both ethically and in terms of the previous owner's biological and genetic history. It's a transaction that never really ends.

The Red Market

Law and economics recognize three types or markets: white, gray, and black. Black markets trade in illegal goods and services like guns and drug running while bootleg DVDs and nontaxed income fall into legal gray areas. White markets are the territory of everything legal and aboveboard—from the groceries that are purchased at a corner bodega to the income taxes that are dutifully filed every year. All three of these markets have two common features: the things being traded have real-world values that can be easily reduced to dollars and cents, and the transactions end the minute money changes hands. Markets in flesh are different because their customers owe their lives and family relationships to the supply chain.

Welcome to the red market.

Red markets are the product of contradictions that arise when social taboos surrounding the human body collide with the individual urge to live a long, happy life. If commodity markets can be figured with algebra, red markets require calculus. Every equation holds both a zero and infinity. Red markets occur on the cusp of major life-changing events for either the supplier or the buyer. Whether the buyer acknowledges it or not, flesh creates a lifelong debt to the person who supplied it.

Because of this bond and because we tend to reject the language of commercialism when dealing with bodies, all red markets also share a curious language of altruism throughout the transaction. Kidneys, blood, and human eggs are "donated," not sold. Adoptive parents take in needy children, they're not adding to the size of their own family.

There are few other transactions that immediately raise ethical red flags as buying parts of other people.

And yet, despite these links, the dollar prices for human bodies and body parts are well established and the supply is, thanks in part to burgeoning populations in impoverished parts of the world, nearly limitless.

In Egypt, India, Pakistan, and the Philippines, entire villages sell organs, rent wombs, and sign away rights to their bodies after death—not only under duress, but also in mutually agreeable transactions. Middlemen who deal in human parts—often hospitals and government institutions, but sometimes the most unscrupulous criminals—buy for the lowest possible price while assuring buyers that the parts come from ethical sources. Though procurement is sometimes abhorrent, the final sale is often legal and usually sanctioned by the implicit moral dimension of saving human lives. The crimes are covered up in a veil of altruistic ideals.

Unlike any other transaction we are likely to make in our lives, buying on the red market makes us indebted to all of the links between the source of parts and the final outcome. There are few other transactions that immediately raise ethical red flags as buying parts of other people. The question of what makes an "ethical source" is one that every potential beneficiary of the red market needs to take seriously.

If we need our body to live, then how can any part of it possibly be spared? In a case of live organ donation, how can a sick person become entitled to the organs of a healthy person? What criteria have to be met to move a child from the third world to the first? Inevitably red markets have the nasty social side effect of moving flesh upward—never downward— through social classes. Even without a criminal element, unrestricted free markets act like vampires, sapping the health and strength from ghettos of poor donors and funneling their parts to the wealthy. . . .

The Ethics of Exchanging Body Parts

For the most part we are comfortable with the idea of buying bodies and body parts as long as we don't really know where they come from. Ideally we would buy human kidneys like we would any other meat in the grocery store: wrapped in plastic and Styrofoam with no hint of the slaughterhouse. At some level we all know that it took a sacrifice to bring a human body to the market, but we just don't want too many details.

Most of us know someone whose life has been saved by an emergency blood transfusion, or a family who has adopted a child from a foreign country. We have probably met people who have benefited from fertility treatments, or who have had their lives extended by an organ transplant. We certainly know doctors who have studied anatomy on real human skeletons; and we have taken drugs that were first tested on human guinea pigs.

It is not bad that these things exist. Some of the most important advances in science have only been made possible precisely because we have treated people as things. Who we are as people depends a lot on who we are as meat. And for the most part we do okay managing the difficult terrain between our physical selves and the part of us that, for lack of a better concept, has a soul.

Criminal and unethical red markets are far smaller than their legitimate counterparts. According to the World Health Organization, about 10 percent of world organ transplants are obtained on the black market. As a rule of thumb, that figure seems to apply to just about every other market for human bodies as well.

The stakes are high. Who we are as a society depends on how we address that remaining 10 percent. Do we let blood brokers and child kidnappers ply their trade and write off the human fallout as just another cost of doing business? The prevalence of kidney brokers in the third world and exploited Eastern European egg sellers in the former Soviet bloc has as much to do with global economic inequalities as it does with the way we manage red markets. Is it even possible to set up a system that minimizes damage across all red markets?

Altruism is simply not a reliable foundation for collecting and distributing human bodies.

Reducing the number of criminals is not only a legal problem; the solution must come from a fundamental reevaluation of our long-held beliefs on the sanctity of the human body, economics, altruism, and privacy. We need to stop viewing the demand for bodies and human tissue as a fixed issue that can only be answered by increasing the overall supply. Instead, the demand for organs, hair, children, and bones is first and foremost a function of overall (and perceived) supply. If bones are freely available in Asia, someone will find a way to make use of them. If more kidneys enter into the market, doctors will deem more people eligible for kidney transplants. The more adoption agencies advertise overcrowded orphanages, the more people will come forward to take the children into their homes. And the more eggs available on the open market, the more people will fly to other countries to receive them. . . .

The Misconception of Altruistic Organ Donation

Even more important, it is impossible to build an economic system that depends on altruism as a source of raw materials. In an ideal world no one would buy or sell another human being—all exchanges of humanity would be based on reciprocity and goodwill to all. That world, however, is not the one we live in. Very few people give away their kidney or eggs, or risk their health in a clinical trial out of pure goodwill. While I do not believe that commercial transactions for human tissue will curtail the existence of black markets, clearly the hypocrisy of using altruism as an excuse to buy cheap raw materials does nothing to serve the greater good. The meager payments granted to the people who sell their bodies merely puts the pressure of selling flesh on people lower down on the social totem pole. . . .

Although it sounds good on paper and on the floor of Congress, altruism is simply not a reliable foundation for collecting and distributing human bodies. At its best it diminishes the incentive for people to supply red markets, and at its worst altruism is a convenient cover story for taking advantage of donors.

The depersonalization of human tissue is one of the broadest failings of modern medicine.

The Need to Personalize Human Organs

Finally, red markets will flourish as long as legal markets in bodies are not transparent. The condition for any ethical human body or tissue exchange depends on absolute transparency of the supply chain.

Even in the best hospitals in the United States, it is almost impossible to know the identity of a brain-dead donor who gave up his or her organs so that another person could live.

Most adoption agencies prefer to keep the identities of the birth parents secret to protect them from uncomfortable questions down the line, and nurses and doctors routinely scrub the names of egg donors off the official paperwork. While the intentions are usually noble, it is far too easy for unethical practitioners to harvest organs from unwilling donors, kidnap children and sell them into the adoption stream, steal blood from prisoners, and coerce women into selling eggs under dangerous conditions. In every case criminals can use the guise of privacy to protect their illicit supply chains.

The depersonalization of human tissue is one of the broadest failings of modern medicine. Our goal in this century should be to integrate and repersonalize human identities into the supply chain. Every bag of blood should include the name of the original donor, every adopted child should have full access to their personal history, and every transplant recipient should know who gave an organ.

This would require a major change in the way we think about the use and reuse of human bodies. Every human has a history that needs to be told as his or her body moves through a red market. We aren't born as neutral products that are by nature reducible to commercial barter. But undoubtedly we all are customers on a red market. The sooner we accept that, the sooner we can do something about it.

And so the same standards that apply to buying used cars should also apply to buying body parts. It isn't legal to sell stolen cars, nor is it legal to sell ones that are sure to break down. Savvy customers always get accident reports before they invest money in a used vehicle. If cars have histories, then so should bodies. Why shouldn't parents be able to check to see if it is possible to locate the parents of the child that they adopted, or someone who bought an egg for implantation check to have access to the medical history of the donor's family? Shouldn't we know whose skeleton hangs in our doctor's closet?

Transparency won't solve every problem. Undoubtedly criminals will be able to forge paperwork, invent new backstories, and disguise unethical practices in new and imaginative ways. International boundaries and changes in legal jurisdictions make it easier for criminals to hide their tracks. However, a clear paper trail makes it easier to flag dangerous operators.

5

The Selling of Body Parts
Could Benefit the Poor

Clark Wolf

*Clark Wolf is a professor of philosophy and director of the bio-
ethics program at Iowa State University.*

*Because there is a shortage of donated human organs, people in
need of transplants die every single day. Many argue that a legitimate market in which human organs are bought and sold
would solve the shortage problem and thus save countless lives.
Critics, however, are concerned that such a market would exploit
the poor who have a greater incentive to sell their organs than
the rich. Those concerned by the injustice of disproportionate
wealth should strive to remedy it rather than prevent someone
from bettering their life through selling an organ.*

In the film *Dirty Pretty Things*, one of the main characters,
Okwe (played by Chiwetel Ejiofor), discovers that his em-
ployer, "Sneaky" (played by Sergi Lopez), is running a peculiar
business. During the day Sneaky seems an ordinary hotelier.
But on the side he runs a service to provide counterfeit passports for illegal immigrants who wish to remain in Britain. He
arranges for poor immigrants to "donate" one of their kidneys, which he sells to people in need of a transplant. In return, he provides the "donors" with forged passports or immi-
gration documents. Unfortunately he employs an incompetent

physician to perform the surgery. We never discover how many of those who participate in Sneaky's scheme die after their kidneys are removed. But what we discover about the procedure gives us reason to believe that few could survive.

In the course of the film, we discover that Okwe is in fact a surgeon from Nigeria. Over time, Okwe finds himself drawn further and further into Sneaky's world: Sneaky uses Okwe's own goodness as a weapon to manipulate him by showing him pictures of a little girl he (Sneaky) says will be saved by the pending kidney transplant. Okwe is also drawn in because of his friendship with a Turkish immigrant, Senay (played by Audrey Tautou), and his concern to protect her from Sneaky's incompetent surgeon. It is Okwe's own virtue that tempts him to participate in Sneaky's scheme. As Okwe's friend Guo Yi (played by Benedict Wong) says, "There's nothing more dangerous than a virtuous man."

Ethical Questions Concerning the Sale of Organs

The film raises many different issues, only some of which will be discussed here. One important issue that occupies center stage is the specific problem of whether it is morally permissible for people to sell and buy transplant organs. While the arrangement described in the film is horrific, some people urge that the main problem with the existing transplant organ system is the *absence* of a legitimate market, rather than the existence of a black market. Another issue addressed in the film is that of commodification or marketization: Are there some things that simply should not be bought and sold on an open market, even when the participants are consenting adults? Can we legitimately prohibit people from selling things they own or control, like their kidneys? Like sex? Finally, there is the problem of exploitation: Sneaky exploits people who are willing to take an enormous risk only because they are desperate. Is their choice to sell their kidneys *voluntary*, or do the circumstances in which the choice is made undermine its freedom? If one judges that the risk of selling her kidney is worth taking, do we nonetheless have a right to interfere? . . .

These donors would be better off if they were able to sell their kidneys than they would be if they were unable to do so.

In 2004, the *New York Times* published a detailed account of an international market that connects poor organ donors with wealthy Americans in need of organ transplants:

> When Alberty José da Silva heard he could make money, lots of money, by selling his kidney, it seemed to him the opportunity of a lifetime. For a desperately ill 48-year-old woman in Brooklyn whose doctors had told her to get a kidney any way she could, it was. At 38, Mr. da Silva, one of 23 children of a prostitute, lives in a slum near the airport here, in a flimsy two-room shack he shares with a sister and nine other people. "As a child, I can remember seven of us sharing a single egg, or living for day after day on just a bit of manioc meal with salt," Mr. da Silva said in an interview. He recalled his mother as a woman who "sold her flesh" to survive. Last year he decided that he would, too. Now, a long scar across his side marks the place where a kidney and a rib were removed in exchange for $6,000, paid by middlemen in an international organ trafficking ring.

The movie *Dirty Pretty Things* is a work of fiction. But the problems it addresses are real problems that real people face every day. Is it morally defensible to allow poor people to sell their organs to rich people? We might object that such arrangements are exploitative in the sense that they take advantage of the unfortunate predicament of the donors. But some might respond that these donors would be better off if they were able to sell their kidneys than they would be if they were unable to do so. Those who accept payment must value the cash more than they value what they're giving up, or else they wouldn't be willing to make the exchange. Are there some things that just shouldn't be bought and sold on the market? And what right do we have to interfere in a voluntary exchange between consenting adults? Should people have a right to decide for themselves which risks they should take and which they should avoid, or do we have a right to intervene and make the decision for them?

Perhaps the reason we prohibit people from selling their kidneys for transplant is that this procedure involves risks for the donor. Still, under most circumstances people are responsible for their own risks, and other people have no right to intervene to prevent them from taking risks they themselves have considered and accepted. If I wish to run risks by biking to work (which involves much greater personal risk than driving a car would), or to spend my leisure time climbing cliffs, the decision is my own. In these cases, you could pay me to take the risk in question without violating the law. But in the United States, if you pay me to have my kidney removed, you (and I) have violated the law. What is the difference between these cases? If the risks are comparable, why do we allow the law to intervene in one case and not in the others? . . .

A Closer Look at Exploitation

Why does Senay consent to trade her kidney for a passport? It is because she is absolutely desperate. Why did Alberty da Silva sell his kidney for six thousand dollars? Because he was very poor and needed the money. It is worth asking whether such exchanges are impermissibly exploitative in the sense that they take advantage of people who are very poor and who would not be willing to put their lives and health at risk if they were not desperate. When Okwe tells Senay "For you and me, there is only survival" he drives home the point that they have few options. Senay's life in London is intolerably bad. She concludes that her only option, the only thing she can do to pursue her hope for a decent life, is to sell her kidney to Sneaky. If people are willing to sell their kidneys only because they have no other options, is their decision even voluntary? In such a situation, is a purchase offer exploitative?

To understand the sense in which these arrangements may be impermissibly exploitative, we need to distinguish between at least two different senses of the term *exploitation*, which will be explored below.

> *E1-Exploitation*: A exploits B when A intentionally causes B to fall into an unfortunate predicament, and then uses B's misfortune as a lever to manipulate B into doing what A wants B to do. . . .

> *Example*: Alph meets Beth at a bar, and she tells him she's planning to drive out into the desert. While she's in the bathroom, Alph sidles out to Beth's car, slashes the spare, and puts a slow leak in one of the tires. Then as Beth heads out for the desert, Alph quietly finishes his beer, planning to go out to find Beth after the tire goes flat and after enough time has passed that her life is in danger from the heat. On finding desperate Beth, Alph offers to sell her his spare provided that she signs over the deed to her house and pays him all the money in her savings account.

The existing black market for kidneys is not E1-exploitative unless those who arrange for the sale of transplant organs intentionally put the prospective donors into the desperate predicament that renders them willing to sell. In the case of Alberty da Silva and others involved in the South African transplant ring discussed above, da Silva's poverty was not caused by those who offered to buy his kidney. And in *Dirty Pretty Things*, the desperation of the poor immigrants who sell their kidneys is not caused by Sneaky; he just takes advantage of their plight. We need another sense of exploitation to identify the problem:

> *E2-Exploitation*: B is in an unfortunate predicament, for which A is not responsible. But A takes advantage of the un-

fortunate predicament of B, using B's misfortune as a lever to manipulate B into doing what A wants B to do.

Once again, an example may make this clear:

Example: Alph is driving through the desert and by chance finds Beth stuck on the road in a desperate and life-threatening situation with a flat tire and no spare. Alph offers to sell Beth his spare tire provided that she signs over the deed to her house and pays Alph all the money in her savings account.

In this case, Alph does not intentionally *cause* Beth's misfortune; he just takes advantage of it. While his offer may save her life, clearly he doesn't deserve any praise for making it. While there is clearly something seriously wrong with arrangements like this one, it does not follow that anyone else has a right to interfere with E2-exploitative arrangements unless they are also willing to do something to improve the predicament of the person who is exploited. Legislative prohibition of E2-exploitative arrangements would certainly be misplaced if the object of such legislation were to improve the situation of the exploited.

One might be inclined to regard Sneaky's exploitation of poor immigrants as E2-exploitation. Sneaky doesn't directly or intentionally cause the poverty and desperation of those he exploits. If their predicament is unjust (as it certainly is), he is no more responsible than others—no more responsible than we are, for example—for the initial injustice that leaves them willing to take an enormous risk. E2-exploitation leaves its victims better off than they would otherwise be. But because his surgeon is incompetent, because Sneaky doesn't care whether the donors live or die, those who sell their kidneys to him are much worse off as a result. So even if we accept the view that third parties usually have no business interfering with E2-exploitative arrangements, it would certainly not follow that we should leave Sneaky to continue to exploit (and murder) his victims.

Improving a Bad Situation

What is peculiar about E2-exploitation is that the exploitative offer actually improves the situation of the person who is exploited. This is not the case for E1-exploitation. If we were to prohibit Alph from selling the tire to Beth in this outrageous offer, as a result she will be even worse off than she already is. Some people take this fact as a conclusive argument that E2-exploitation is not unfair to those who are exploited. Thus, Sally Satel writes, in the *New York Times*:

> Some critics worry that compensation for kidney donation by the living would be most attractive to the poor and hence exploit them. But if it were government-regulated we could ensure that donors would receive education about their choices, undergo careful medical and psychological screening and receive quality follow-up care. We could even make a donation option that favors the well-off by rewarding donors with a tax credit. Besides, how is it unfair to poor people if compensation enhances their quality of life? . . .

How is it unfair to poor people if compensation enhances their quality of life?

Ideally, we might wish to provide Mr. da Silva with opportunities that his life does not now present. Arguably, justice requires that we do this. But if we are unable to address the underlying injustice that caused his poverty and the poverty of millions of others like him, then we are not justified in stepping in to prevent him from exercising the problematic opportunity that presented itself to him—the opportunity to sell his kidney in a problematic and (probably) exploitative arrangement. If he is appropriately informed about the risks involved, if he nonetheless judges that the risk associated with donating a kidney is worth six thousand dollars to him, who are we to tell him that he is making the wrong choice? Unless we are willing to step in and eliminate the initial injustice that leaves him in a situation where he is willing to accept this problematic offer, we have no right to prevent him from improving his situation by accepting such an offer.

6

The Selling of Body Parts Does Not Benefit the Poor

Karen A. Hudson

Karen A. Hudson is a recent graduate of the University of Oregon Robert D. Clark Honors College and is interested in clinical psychology.

The international black market organ trade, in which body parts are considered valuable commodities, exploits the poor and creates communities of disabled people. The competitive nature of this market has led organ brokers to search out people who are in such debt-ridden and poverty-stricken situations that they will sell their organs as a means to survive. Because these so-called "donors" often do not receive medical care before and after the removal of an organ, they become ill, unable to go back to work, and thus become even more impoverished. Significant changes in the organ trade must be developed to protect organ donors from such unethical exploitation; education about the risks involved and proper medical care would be of great benefit.

Despite the condemnation of selling organs, which dates back to a 1985 World Medical Association statement and principles forbidding commercial transactions relating to "the human body and its parts" set forth by the World Health Organization in 1991, money still exchanges hands for harvested organs on the black market. It is estimated that 10% of the

63,000 annual kidney transplants involve payment to a non-related donor of a different nationality, and this statistic not only highlights the practice of paying for organs, which is illegal in many countries, but introduces the international aspect of the organ trade. Considering that a kidney can be bought from a donor for $1,000–3,000, and can be sold for up to $40,000, it is apparent that a huge market-driven divide exists between those involved in a transaction on which livelihoods are based. This discrepancy between the donor's compensation and the ultimate market value of a kidney is a product of the competitive, profit-focused market economy encouraged by globalization.

Taking from the Poor and Giving to the Rich

Nancy Scheper-Hughes is a member of Organs Watch, a human rights group operating out of the University of California, Berkeley. The purpose of this organization is to investigate rumors, complaints, and allegations involving the trafficking of organs, human rights violations regarding the acquisition of organs, and related issues. In her report ["The End of the Body: The Global Traffic in Organs for Transplant Surgery"] published on the Organs Watch website, Scheper-Hughes notes how organ transplantation follows "modern routes of capital," "from third world to first world, from poor to rich bodies, from black to brown to white bodies." As globalization promotes a market economy, the competitive nature of this market is reflected in many facets of society, including a nation's healthcare system. The currency of the exchange, be it in dollars or organs, often flows as Scheper-Hughes describes. As an example, [Michael] Davidson [in "Universal Design: The Work of Disability in an Age of Globalization"] refers to when Bayer sold large quantities of a blood-clotting factor to Asia and Latin America, because the product was not fit for sale in the United States or Europe. The result of this transaction was an HIV infection rate of 90% among those targeted by the company, and a profit of four million dollars for Bayer. This is an example of money flowing out of developing nations to wealthier ones in a global economy and at a cost to the developing nation. When this occurs in the context of the organ trade, the results are similar—the exploitation of those without money and resources by those with money and resources.

Lawrence Cohen, in a discussion about "kidney zones" in India, illustrates how social hierarchy and corporate competition interact to produce areas where the organ trade flourishes. He hypothesizes that "kidney zones" (areas where kidneys are sold in large numbers) "emerge through interactions between surgical entrepreneurs, persons facing extraordinary debt, and medical brokers." Globalization has brought the once rare procedure of organ transplantation, before carried out only in developed nations, to countries around the world. This set the stage for the competition between public and private healthcare entities, and in combination with surgeons willing to take risks for money and a pool of indebted citizens willing to do whatever it takes to keep their family afloat, the organ trade thrives.

In Brazil, the competitive economic pressures of a market-based economy have contributed to a healthcare system that fuels the supply and demand of organ trading. As discussed by Scheper-Hughes, there exists outside the free national healthcare system a private medical sector, resulting in a competition for organs between free health clinics and private ones. She also explains that the financial incentives are much higher in the private sector, and so it is the private clinics that are more aggressive about obtaining organs so that they can charge more—and thus profit more—from transplant surgeries. Of course, it is possible that the organs obtained are legitimately donated, but evidence exists of police investigations into the so-called "body mafia" that suggests otherwise. This group of criminals has links with hospital and ambulance staff, as well as within the police force in an underground ring designed to trade human organs. In this example, the flow of money remains in the country, but those who prosper are a select few, and those on waiting lists in public hospitals may be skipped over as newly available organs go to wealthy private clients.

Donors often have little or no access to hospital care following the extraction of an organ.

In 2007, China introduced a new set of regulations in an attempt to crack down on the sale of organs. China is a unique example of the hierarchical flow of organs and money, as it is the only country that uses the organs of executed prisoners for organ transplantation. There has been much advocacy against this practice by international human rights activists, but China has held out. Why continue the internationally rejected practice of harvesting organs from executed prisoners? Perhaps because China has become a mecca for wealthy foreigners in need of transplants and who are capable of paying up to $30,000 for an organ. With the Chinese healthcare system becoming increasingly market-driven, hospitals are under significant pressure to generate income, and therefore ask fewer ethical questions about the sources of the organs.

Generating Impoverished Disabled People

To better understand Scheper-Hughes' flowchart model of organs and capital, one must differentiate between the disabled parties involved in the organ trade. Effects of globalization affect two separate categories of people, both of which may identify as having disabilities. The first category consists of those in need of an organ, which can be further divided into wealthy private clientele and the locals who are often skipped over to serve these wealthier individuals. The second category is composed of those who sell their organs. This group of "donors" is most drastically exploited by economic and health-care systems. These people are impaired due to the extraction of an organ and disabled because they are often left in debt and may be unable to be a productive member of society due to a lack of proper medical care, both preceding and following the removal of an organ. . . .

Donors often have little or no access to hospital care following the extraction of an organ, which is necessary to prevent complications after surgery. A woman in Pakistan donated a kidney to support her family after her husband was unable to work after an accident, but her health became worse after the donation because she received no post-operative care. Documentation on poor organ recipients in Brazil showed that they were unable to afford the costly immunosuppressant therapy to prevent organ rejection, and had to pool and taper their doses prematurely, as one month of the immunosuppressant drug costs more than most of those families earn in a month. These impoverished recipients are forced to choose between maintaining their health and plummeting (possibly further) into debt. Though the donation of an organ in itself might not constitute a disability, being unable to work and live a healthy life because of a lack of available medical care following organ extraction does.

Using Body Parts to Pay Off Debts

The "donors" of the organs going to those wait-listed locals and wealthy travelers are the crux of disability and the black market organ trade. I will refer to these individuals as organ "donors," but note that such a term denotes a voluntariness that is brought into question with the following arguments, as well as a false implication of no compensation for the "donors." However, I will use "donor" as a critical commentary on the continual denial of the role globalization is playing to worsen the situations of those in a position to "donate" their organs; primarily, how globalization is failing to address the issue of debt on the part of the donor, and the resulting acceptance of the use of body parts as currency to pay off these debts.

Organs are seen as another form of collateral for debt-collectors.

Cohen, in his time spent in India studying the organ trade, summarizes the plight of kidney donors. The theme running through each story he heard was that of debt and poverty. Scheper-Hughes makes the statement, "A market price—even a fair one—on body parts exploits the desperation of the poor." This is a desperation coming out of debt-ridden and poverty-stricken situations, even culminating in newspaper ads offering to sell body parts. A major paper in Brazil ran an ad "offering to sell any organ of my body that is not vital to my survival and which could help save another person's life in exchange for an amount of money that will allow me to feed my family." A woman in Bangladesh placed an ad in the Sunday paper to sell one of her eyes in order to pay rent and feed her daughter. This problem of debt drives organ donations, but does not disappear once a body part has been sold. All of the donors with whom Cohen spoke were back in debt despite having sold a kidney, possibly related to issues linked to their social status. Problems relating to social status are often related to oppression within a given system, reflecting less on the struggling individual and more on the system in which he or she lives.

The organ trade has also changed the way bodies are seen by debt-collectors. The image of the mafia breaking the legs of someone who borrowed money is a familiar one, but in places like India, organs are seen as another form of collateral for debt-collectors. This expectation that body parts can and should be traded for currency is also reflected in the thought processes of those in debt, as evidenced by the newspaper ads and the information compiled by Cohen about poverty as a common theme of donors. In Pakistan, often those who donate kidneys have no other way to make money because they live in a bonded labor system, tied to property owned by those financially better off. Without the means of production, these Pakistanis sell their organs in an attempt to liberate themselves from this oppressive debt bondage.

Disregarding the Needs of Donors

There have been a number of suggestions to improve conditions for organ donors in attempts to prevent individuals from becoming a disabled product of the organ trade. Cohen notes that no data exist on the long-term effects of kidney extractions, despite doctors insisting that risk is minimal. If studies could be done to examine the longitudinal effects of donating a kidney or other organ, donors could be more informed about their decisions. These studies would be particularly beneficial if conducted in situations outside the typical medical model of affluent white donors altruistically giving up kidneys to relatives in developed nations, as this typical situation is not the "typical" experience of those exploited by the organ trade. Knowing the risks, both physically and in regard to ending up back in debt, might not realistically make a difference for someone in as desperate of a situation as Cohen and Scheper-Hughes describe, but the effort going into such a project would raise awareness of pertinent issues. This process would work towards combating the silence Davidson describes between globalization and disability.

There has also been significant effort put into developing measures that can be used to aid in the decision-making of an organ recipient that includes five supposedly quantifiable measures representing "burden of disease," and this measure is designed to help a possible organ recipient decide if he or she wants to go through with the transplant and to further educate the recipient about the nature of his or her situation and possible outcomes. The development of this measure illustrates the amount of focus placed on the organ recipient instead of the donor, despite the fact that such research could be used as a framework for donor decision-making as well. The constant refusal to acknowledge the needs of the organ donors—from simply investing time in gathering and conveying accurate and comprehensive information to addressing underlying societal problems of class hierarchies—is a significant problem.

Poverty and deprivation sustain the trade in human organs.

It is today's system of globalization that disregards the needs of impoverished individual donors both before and after organ transplantations, in turn creating an international community of disabled people. The imposition of economic structures that fuel competition between private corporations and public entities (such as hospitals) only compounds already present inequalities and hierarchies in developing nations. Experts advocate developing clear regulations for healthcare systems on a global scale and shifting the focus to preventative medicine to avoid problems that lead to organ failure, but if these changes are made under the same systems that are praising globalization as we know it, then they might not really be changes at all. The disabled community entering into the organ trade, and those who are products of it, would greatly benefit from structural changes in society that work to break down class hierarchies, providing support for those in poverty and making healthcare available that is of the same quality as that received by the wealthy. Such changes could very well be brought about through the process of globalization, but not as globalization is progressing today. The black market organ trade itself could be curbed with proper advancements addressing the conditions of the donors, because, as an Indian report on the ethical considerations of the organ trade noted: "In the final analysis, poverty and deprivation sustain the trade in human organs."

7

The Sperm Donor Market Raises Ethical Concerns

Jeff Stryker

Jeff Stryker is a writer who specializes in health policy and bioethics.

The market for donor sperm—also known as sperm banks—is a thriving business, yet is largely unregulated in the United States. These sperm banks are not required to keep records regarding the numbers of births, track the health of donors, make genetic information available to children born of donor insemination, or limit how many children an individual donor can procreate. As a result, many Americans have ethical concerns regarding the best interests of the children. For example, do children have the right to know their ancestral heritage? Whether they have half siblings? Any genetic disorders? Do they even have the right to learn the truth about their conception? Parents, donors, journalists, regulators, physicians all have differing opinions; many call for regulation, others think government interference would be a bad idea. The important thing is that more people are becoming aware of the medical and ethical issues involved.

Assisted reproduction was born in shame and secrecy. In 1884, Philadelphia physician William Pancoast performed an experiment on a female patient whose husband was infertile. Without asking her or her husband's permission, he inseminated his patient while she was under anesthesia. The semen came from the "most handsome" of his medical students (although it was later speculated to be Dr. Pancoast's own). Eventually, he disclosed his experiment to the husband, but the woman never discovered the real origins of the child she bore.

A Serious Lack of Record-Keeping

Only now, more than 100 years later, is third-party reproduction beginning to shake off this aura as policy changes roil the field in Europe and new attitudes begin to lap up on American shores. In the United States, the U.S. Food and Drug Administration requires that donors be tested for diseases such as HIV and hepatitis while their sperm are frozen and quarantined, only to be released six months later when certified disease free. But today's "sperm banks" are under no obligation to report numbers of births, place any limits on births to individual donors, track the health of donors, or make information available to children born of donor insemination.

This poses some serious scientific, medical, and ethical questions. Should individual men be able to procreate perhaps hundreds of children anonymously? Over the long haul, what does this mean for human genetic diversity? What about genetic diseases? And should children "fathered" via sperm banks be allowed to know who their father is? These are questions that are only now being asked—despite the long history of "artificial insemination," as it was once quaintly called—not just in the United States but also abroad. The answers, as we shall see, are as controversial as the questions. . . .

Today, approximately two dozen commercial sperm banks operate in the United States. An untold number are also associated with university fertility clinics, banking sperm for pre-vasectomy and pre-chemotherapy and radiation treatment patients—no one keeps track of how many. Nor can it be said with any certainty how many children are born each year as a result of donor insemination, although the most frequently cited guesstimates range between 30,000 to 50,000. . . .

And who are the sperm donors? Some are young men depositing sperm in anticipation of their own future infertility, including those about to go off to war. But the vast majority of donors—or perhaps more accurately, sperm vendors—are men who sell their semen for $40 to $60 per "donation." No longer are donors almost exclusively medical men, though doctor semen remains in great demand. Education is still a highly sought-after attribute, with sperm banks seeking donors through advertisements in college newspapers.

If sperm donor is a misleading tag, sperm banking is not, at least insofar as it suggests a profit-seeking commercial enterprise. Market forces shape how the supply of sperm meets the demand. In the early days of sperm banking, race, hair color, and eye color were typically the only traits revealed. Nowadays, buyers still seek sperm of certain ethnicity and physical characteristics; taller men are the rule, no shorties need apply. . . .

Although sperm banking is now a vital part of this new frontier of baby making, the industry remains largely unregulated in the United States. In other countries, fundamental changes are being wrought in sperm banking practices. Canada and Britain now ban payment to sperm donors. Britain, Sweden, Austria, the Netherlands, and parts of Australia no longer permit anonymous donation, insisting that donors be available to be contacted by their children when the offspring reach adulthood. Some of these countries are establishing registries to help make this possible. These restrictions were put in place despite concerns they could dry up the pool of willing donors.

Occasional sperm bank scandals have brought episodic attention to the state-wide industry, if not much reform. When Cecil Jacobson, the renowned physician and infertility specialist, was discovered in the early 1980s to have inseminated as many as 75 women coming to his Virginia clinic with his own sperm (unbeknownst to them), prosecutors weren't sure he had committed any crime. He was eventually convicted of 52 counts of mail fraud, wire fraud, and perjury and served time in federal prison, losing his medical license.

The Debate About Regulation and Registries

Such occasional scandals are outliers, say the bankers, not cause for further regulation. "More regulation of sperm banking is a solution in search of a problem," says Sean Tipton, a Washington, D.C.-based spokesperson for the American Society of Reproductive Medicine, which is headquartered in Birmingham, Alabama. "The danger with more regulation, like more genetic testing or changing the rules about anonymity, is that you give up important autonomy and privacy at great economic expense. It is not clear what you gain."

Wendy Kramer, a Colorado single mother and founder of the Internet-based Donor Sibling Registry [DSR], doesn't agree. She is perhaps sperm banking's most vocal and visible critic. "Sure, there is some regulation at the front door, screening the men who come in," she concedes. "But what about afterwards, when the births occur? No one in the industry cares by then."

Kramer was inspired by her son to found the Donor Sibling Registry as a Yahoo users' group chat room seven years ago. Her son Ryan, now a handsome 17-year-old in his fourth year of college studying aeronautical engineering at the University of Colorado at Boulder, was eager to find any half-siblings. In fact, Ryan's curiosity was even more precocious. At age two she recalls him asking, "Is my Dad dead, or what?"

Wendy Kramer conceived her son Ryan with sperm from a local bank in Colorado. "The lady at the bank just suggested a sample from someone who looked like my husband." (She's now divorced.) "I suppose I got the 'high octane,'" she joked, proudly sharing stories about her bright young son's college career.

DSR has grown from a chat room into a thriving website. At last count, the registry had more than 9,000 registered members, including parents of donor-inseminated children, some children themselves and donors who post their donor numbers and profiles to facilitate matches with families of their offspring. More than 3,800 matches have been made with half siblings or donor fathers.

The sperm-banking industry tends to dismiss the yearning to find genetic heritage.

After six and a half years of searching, Ryan Kramer found a half sister and was match number 2,910. "This little 13-year-old girl was just beside herself to have an older brother," says Ms. Kramer. "I don't try to define their relationship. They're teenagers. They 'IM' [instant message] each other," says Ms. Kramer.

A Concern About Genetic Disorders

The sperm-banking industry tends to dismiss the yearning to find genetic heritage and the worrying stories from DSR match ups as "anecdotal." Says ASRM [American Society for Reproductive Medicine] spokesperson Sean Tipton: "I don't draw any conclusions from the Donor Sibling Registry. I don't know if there is any counterpart organization for happy children of sperm donors."

But even if data is not the plural of anecdotes, some of the anecdotes are enough to give one pause. Medical concerns in particular are a frequent topic of discussion when families get together on the Donor Sibling Registry. As will be detailed further below, one set of families discovered that five different children born of the same donor were all autistic. Other parents of donor children suffering from genetic diseases have found half siblings sharing the same illness.

Yet sperm banks have frequently refused to contact other potentially affected children, track down the donor, or even pull the sperm from the shelf. . . .

Concern about unwitting transmission of genetic disorders from sperm donors to many more children than would be possible in conventional families is one factor driving calls for more disclosure, traceability, and limits on the numbers of children born to a particular donor. Consider Ben, a 29-year-old practicing lawyer who masturbated his way through a Washington, D.C.,-area law school, earning about $30,000 to help pay for tuition.

Ben asked that we not publish his last name because he's not ready for the whole world, including his professional colleagues, to know about his donor career. He explains that he saw the anguish two cousins endured trying to get pregnant, struggling through many expensive cycles of in vitro fertilization. He figured his sperm donations could help people experience the joy of parenthood, while helping to finance law school.

The question of whether to require identity release . . . is perhaps the hottest topic in sperm banking.

"It wasn't exactly hard work," Ben quipped in a recent phone interview. Yet as a frequent depositor at his local sperm bank, he may have spread more joy than he reckoned.

Ben, explains Wendy Kramer, is one of her "brave donors," who posted his story with his donor number on the Donor Sibling Registry and permits contact from families who have purchased his sperm. Ben now uses an Excel spreadsheet to manage relationships with the families of his 28—count 'em, 28—donor offspring.

"It is just easier not to mix them up that way," he says. Ben is only a few years out of law school. His dozens of kids are still of pre-school age. Most of the contact from parents involves email questions about his health status and genetic history. . . .

The Dispute Between Privacy and Identity Disclosure

The question of whether to require identity release—that is, to allow children to contact their donor father when they come of age—is perhaps the hottest topic in sperm banking.

Ellen Singer, a social worker and adoption program specialist with The Center for Adoption Support and Education, Inc., a non-profit organization with three offices in Maryland, says that sperm banking lags far behind the adoption field in terms of regulation and oversight. "There are still professionals who advise parents not to tell their children that they were a result of donor insemination or donor eggs," she says.

But views are evolving. Singer sees disclosure as a human rights issue. "Kids need to know the truth about their conception," she argues. "That doesn't mean the whole world has to know, but the kids should."

But Singer empathizes with parents who worry about stigma. "The secrecy can be well-meaning and intended to protect the children," she says. "But children don't need protection, they need the truth and ways to cope with the challenges that come with it." The American Society for Reproductive Medicine now advises parents to disclose to their children the details of their conception, even though it opposes more regulation of the industry.

Some sperm banks have been factoring in those privacy vs. disclosure issues for some time now. The Sperm Bank of California, a non-profit outfit established in Berkeley to cater to a largely lesbian clientèle, has offered identity-release semen for more than 20 years. That means the first children born with the option to contact their donor when they turn 18 are now coming of age—and some are beginning to do so.

U.S. sperm banks are increasingly offering donor identity-release sperm as an option. "It goes faster and costs more," says Lisa Jean Moore, who teaches at Purchase College, State University of New York. Moore is a former board president of The Sperm Bank of California. She is also the parent of two daughters, one born with sperm supplied by a friend, the other with sperm purchased from a bank.

But not everyone thinks imposing more regulations is a good idea. Gays and lesbians, as well as single mothers by choice, may have some misgivings about how sperm banking operates, but many are nevertheless wary of opening the door to regulators who may have much more cramped notions of what should constitute a family. A lesbian couple from Colorado who found out on DSR that their daughter has more than two dozen half siblings emailed the author to say:

> We would not support government regulation at any level. The government has a history of discrimination against LGBT [lesbian, gay, bisexual and transgendered] families and individuals, and we would not want to open the door to the government prohibiting sales or contributions from LGBT people.

The Best Interests of the Children

As journalist Liza Mundy writes in her wide-ranging *Everything Conceivable: How Assisted Reproduction is Changing Men, Women and the World* (2007), crafting progressive policies is a challenge in this field. "[I]n this area of reproductive science, 'progressive' is a nard concept to pin down." Indeed, almost everyone connected in any way to the field of assisted reproduction gives lip service to the "best interests of the children," even though sperm banks are set up to meet the needs of doctors, patients and parents.

But, in practice, children's best interests can be notoriously difficult to pin down. Who knows what is in the best interest of children born to sperm donors? Clinicians? Regulators? Parents? What about the children themselves?

Deborah Spar, a professor at the Harvard Business School, has examined sperm banking as part of a larger look at the reproductive marketplace, including the practices of buying and selling sperm and eggs, renting wombs, and brokering adoptions. Spar, the author of *The Baby Business: How Money, Science, and Politics Drive the Commerce of Conception* (2006), says she attributes the lack of political interest in regulating sperm banks to the relatively small size of the industry, politicians' reluctance to enter the fray of reproductive decision making, and a general squeamishness about semen.

"No one likes saying the word sperm," she explains. "Plus, the egg extraction process is surgical, but the sperm extraction process is sexual."

Still, Spar believes such squeamishness will give way to calls for more regulation, and does not buy the argument that "as soon as you let the government in they'll be saying that only heterosexuals can have children." She says "there are lots and lots of places to stop along the spectrum between no government regulation and the government telling me when I should have my child and what I should name him."

Besides, a new vocal constituency for reform is about to come of age. "It is going to be the sperm babies who are going to push for donor identification and recordkeeping," Spar predicts. "That is what is going to spur a political debate and wake people up to the medical issues involved."

8

China's Organ Market Is Unethical

S. Elizabeth Forsythe

S. Elizabeth Forsythe, a fellow at the John Jay Institute for Faith, Society, and Law, is a student at the University of Virginia School of Law.

Evidence shows that China conducts more organ transplants than any other country except the United States, yet many Chinese are opposed to organ donation because of cultural traditions. So where are the donated organs coming from? Investigations and eyewitness accounts have reported that the Chinese government harvests organs from executed prisoners without their prior consent. Similar reports accuse the Chinese government of detaining followers of the nonviolent spiritual Falun Gong movement to obtain organs for the lucrative transplant market. Although China claims that its organ transplant program is legal and ethical, people should regard with skepticism China's organ donation procedures.

For millions of ailing Chinese patients awaiting organ transplants, the creation of an orderly and transparent system for managing donation and transplantation could be a great boon. But the recent announcement that China's government is implementing such a system should be eyed skeptically, as the country's record on issues of organ harvesting and donation is pitted with deception and empty promises.

S. Elizabeth Forsythe, "China's Organ Market: A Tale of Prisoners, Tourists, and Lies," *New Atlantis*, Summer 2009, pp. 121–124. Copyright © 2009 by the New Atlantis. All rights reserved. Reproduced by permission.

The organ "shortages" common in other countries are exacerbated in China by traditions about death: the beliefs that a dead body must remain intact before burial to be ensured eternal rest and that death occurs only when breathing ceases and the heart stops beating; the condition of "brain death" is not recognized by Chinese culture. As a result, many Chinese are highly suspicious of and even fundamentally opposed to organ harvesting and transplantation. Without an established transplantation system, and with cultural norms opposed to organ donation, some degree of confusion surrounding transplantation is to be expected.

Allegations of Harvesting Organs from Executed Prisoners

But the problems in China are worse than shortages and confusion. Allegations first surfaced around 1990 that organs were being harvested from executed Chinese prisoners. That year, the London *Guardian* quoted several eyewitnesses attesting to the practice of collecting prisoners' organs immediately after execution. The eyewitnesses asked to remain anonymous out of fear of reprisal; the Chinese government had allegedly insisted that doctors keep the practice a secret. Other newspapers in the early 1990s began uncovering the apparent sale of kidneys to Australian patients in Hong Kong hospitals. Writing in the *Sydney Morning Herald* in 1991, Yojana Sharma noted that

> it is impossible to prove beyond reasonable doubt that Chinese kidneys have been obtained ethically. China insists that the consent of relatives is obtained for the removal of condemned prisoners' organs. But this is impossible to verify. And in the mid-1980s it was common for poor peasants to sell their kidneys for cash, although the Chinese government claims this is no longer the case.

Doctors and government officials in Hong Kong (then still under British rule) had reportedly become suspicious of the growing organ trade between Hong Kong hospitals and China.

Human rights organizations became suspicious, too. In the years following the 1989 Tiananmen Square massacre, Amnesty International noted an increase in China's application of the death penalty, and in 1992 reported on the use of executed prisoners' kidneys without their consent. Human Rights Watch in 1994 reported that, while the Chinese executions originally drove the organ trade, eventually the situation flipped: the demand for organs led to rushed executions of prisoners whose guilt was not unequivocally established, as well as the collection of organs without consent and the use of illegal methods of execution for the sake of preserving the desired organs. Dr. Ronald D. Guttman, a McGill University professor respected for his expertise in transplant science and practice, showed in a 1992 paper that, after 1989, about 90 percent of China's transplanted kidneys came from executed prisoners.

The Chinese government denied all these allegations until 1994, when the Ministry of Health admitted that some organs *were* being taken from executed prisoners—but supposedly never without the prisoners' consent, and executions were never rushed to obtain organs. The ministry called such allegations "baseless," "sheer fabrications," and "vicious slander against China's legal system." That essentially remains the ministry's position today.

China had been killing practitioners of Falun Gong specifically to harvest their organs.

Persecuting Falun Gong Followers to Obtain Organs

The Chinese government has also repeatedly denied similar allegations related to the treatment of Falun Gong adherents. A nonviolent, apolitical spiritual movement based on meditation and exercise, Falun Gong emerged in the early 1990s—coincidental with the rapid expansion of the Chinese organ market. The movement attracted millions of followers until the late 1990s when its growth made Chinese authorities uneasy. In 1998, the Ministry of Public Security began investigating Falun Gong, publicly declaring it a socially disruptive, dangerous, and heretical cult. The next year, the government formally banned Falun Gong and began cracking down on its practitioners, harassing and arresting them. Before long, accusations of persecution and torture surfaced, and by 2001, an op-ed in the *Washington Post* voiced suspicions about a possible link between, on one hand, "the grotesque harvesting and sale of human organs from freshly killed Chinese prisoners" and, on the other hand, "the escalating number of death sentences in China for even nonviolent offenses" as well as curious reports of hundreds of Falun Gong practitioners dying "by 'accident' or 'suicide'" while in prison. Evidence for this link trickled in over the next few years—including purported eyewitness accounts of a secret underground detention center in which Chinese doctors were harvesting organs from Falun Gong prisoners—but the Chinese denied everything.

On July 1, 2006, China outlawed the purchase and sale of human organs, as well as the harvesting of organs without consent. A few days later, David Kilgour, a former Secretary of State for the Canadian government, and David Matas, a Canadian international human rights lawyer, published a report showing that China had been killing practitioners of Falun Gong specifically to harvest their organs. Kilgour and Matas assembled eyewitness accounts, documentary evidence, damning interviews, and suspicious statistics. They noticed, among other aberrations, that China conducts more organ transplants than any other country except for the United States— but that the small number of living donors and brain-dead donors cannot mathematically have been the source of all of the transplanted organs. Stranger still, the average waiting time for a transplanted organ in China is very short—often just a week or two for "transplant tourists" visiting from foreign lands—suggesting "the existence of a large bank of live prospective 'donors.'"

On the weight of the evidence, Kilgour and Matas concluded that

> the government of China and its agencies in numerous parts of the country, in particular hospitals but also detention centers and "people's courts," since 1999 have put to death a large but unknown number of Falun Gong prisoners of conscience. Their vital organs, including kidneys, livers, corneas, and hearts, were seized involuntarily for sale at high prices, sometimes to foreigners, who normally face long waits for voluntary donations of such organs in their home countries.

Attempting to Establish Legitimacy

A few months after the publication of the Kilgour-Matas report, the Chinese Ministry of Health admitted that the great majority of the organs used in transplants in recent years had come from executed prisoners, and put the blame on the rise of transplant tourism: "The current big shortfall of organ donations can't meet demand." (To this day, the Chinese government continues to deny the allegations regarding Falun Gong prisoners' organs.)

Since then, China has sought to give the impression of regulating organ transplantation. In 2007, for instance, the government set medical standards for transplantation and established fines and other punishments for violators—and in 2008, the Ministry of Health claimed to have penalized three hospitals for illegally selling human organs. However, the hospitals were not named and the punishments have not been publicly announced.

The government has also sought to establish standards for organ donation procedures and to encourage Chinese citizens to donate their organs. The Ministry of Health and the Red

Cross Society of China have been jointly developing a national organ registration system, in hopes that national standardization will encourage voluntary donations; they promise to roll out the new system soon. These plans garnered favorable international headlines in 2008 and again in 2009, but there are few real indications of action.

Given China's track record of dissembling and delay, and given the scale of the illegal but lucrative transplant tourism market, there is little reason to expect that the Chinese government will act quickly on its promises of regulation or that it will vigorously enforce the laws now in place. For the foreseeable future, foreigners traveling to China for a transplant should understand that the organs they receive are likely to have been taken under questionable circumstances from inmates, perhaps Falun Gong prisoners, executed by a dishonest and unscrupulous regime.

9

Iran's Organ Vending System Is Beneficial

Benjamin E. Hippen

Benjamin E. Hippen, a transplant nephrologist, is an at-large member of the United Network for Organ Sharing/Organ Procurement and Transplant Network Ethics Committee and serves as an associate editor of the American Journal of Transplantation.

Iran is the only country that has a legal human organ procurement system that provides payment to organ donors. This market system has solved the country's organ shortage and thus saved countless lives, and at the same time has eliminated the problems associated with organ trafficking that many other countries—including the United States—have to deal with. Although serious concerns exist regarding Iran's organ market, such as long-term health outcomes for donors and recipients, the United States can learn valuable lessons from Iran's example with regard to solving America's own organ shortage.

Insofar as the kidney procurement system in Iran can be characterized as a "market," it is a highly standardized and regulated market with only modest room for negotiation. Once potential kidney recipients are identified, they are evaluated by kidney transplant teams, including transplant nephrologists and transplant surgeons. Recipients are coun-

Benjamin E. Hippen, "Organ Sales and Moral Travails: Lessons from the Living Kidney Vendor Program in Iran," *Policy Analysis*, vol 614, March 20, 2008.

seled that it is in their best interest to identify a biologically related living donor. If no biologically related living donor is available or willing to donate, the recipient is referred to the Dialysis and Transplant Patients Association [DATPA]. From there, disposition of the recipient depends on whether the transplant center has an active deceased-donor program. For example, at a major university hospital in Zhiraz, which has an active deceased-donor program, recipients referred to DATPA must generally wait six months for a deceased-donor kidney (though some recipients elect to circumvent this requirement by traveling to Tehran for transplantation). If the recipient does not receive a transplant from a deceased donor after six months, DATPA identifies an immunologically compatible kidney vendor for the recipient.

By 1999 the waiting list for kidney transplants in Iran had been eliminated, a success no other country can claim.

How the Iranian System Works

DATPA is staffed by volunteers with ESRD [end-stage renal disease] and receives no remuneration for matching kidney vendors with recipients. Neither the transplant center nor transplant physicians are involved in identifying potential vendors. Instead, vendors express their own interest in participating by contacting DATPA. Once identified, vendors are referred to the transplant center and evaluated according to the same medical standards applied to living donors who are *not* financially compensated, including the evaluating physician's right to use his medical discretion to veto a vendor's candidacy.

Vendors are paid in two ways. First, the Iranian government provides a fixed compensation to the vendor of approximately $1,200 plus limited health insurance coverage, which currently extends to one year after the exchange and covers only conditions deemed related to the surgery. Second, the vendor receives separate remuneration either from the recipient or, if the recipient is impoverished, from one of a series of designated charitable organizations; this amount is usually between $2,300 and $4,500. The amount and source of the second remuneration is arranged beforehand by DATPA. It is important to note that noncitizens are not eligible to participate in the Iranian organ procurement system as either vendors or recipients. As with dialysis, the Iranian government assumes the cost of treatment, including the kidney procurement, transplant surgery, immunosuppression medications, and postoperative care of the vendor and recipient. Thus, while the Iranian market in organs is heavily regulated, it does allow people to receive several forms of compensation for their organs, including financial compensation.

Unlike the rest of the world, and the United States in particular, the Iranians have found a way to solve their organ shortage; and although their market system is not without problems, it clearly has advantages over other organ procurement systems, primarily that thousands in need do not die while waiting for a compatible donor.

Merits of the Iranian System

Permitting legal organ vending has brought the greatest benefit: By 1999 the waiting list for kidney transplants in Iran had been eliminated, a success no other country can claim. In addition, the Iranians have found a way to minimize the potential negative impact of financial incentives. DATPA serves as an alternative to the for-profit organ brokers who are such a pernicious feature of illegal organ trafficking in other countries. Exchanges by freelance brokers (particularly where legal protections against coercion or fraud are inconsistently enforced) can create incentives for both the broker and the vendor to be untruthful if disclosures might thwart the exchange. For example, if a vendor has a communicable infectious disease, or has kidney disease, there are clear disincentives to identify, discover, or disclose such facts in a system that does not enforce organ brokerage contracts. The Iranian system addresses this problem by making the intermediary a nonprofit, patient-run service organization that trades on the moral commitment of patients to help others in a position similar to their own. That, in turn, provides as powerful a motivation to avoid harmful practices as a system that consistently and strictly enforces laws against coercion and fraud, which redounds to the benefit of vendors.

The Iranians have reduced the possibility that organ vendors will be taken advantage of.

The Iranian not-for-profit, charity-based system also provides a convenient intermediary between the organ vendor and the patient or transplant center, thus mitigating a host of potentially difficult, moral conflicts of interest. Separating the role of identifying vendors from the role of evaluating their medical, surgical, and psychological suitability permits transplant professionals to avoid confusing judgment on a vendor's candidacy with various financial and professional incentives to perform more transplants. Without dwelling on which potential conflicts of interest might evolve into actual conflicts of interest, it is clear that systemwide separation between identifying and screening potential vendors has the advantage of reducing potential concerns.

The Iranians have eliminated their waiting list for kidneys by allowing a limited market in live-donor kidney vending, and in so doing they have discovered a way to minimize some of the perceived dangers of such a system. With DATPA acting as intermediary, the Iranians have reduced the possibility that organ vendors will be taken advantage of by either overzealous middlemen, procurement institutions, or physicians desperate to help their patients. Despite those successes, however, the Iranian system is not without problems.

Concerns with the Iranian System

Both proponents and opponents of kidney vending from the living have reason to be skeptical about the veracity of outcomes reported by Iranian transplant professionals. Precautions must be taken to carefully parse out sound conclusions from those that lack sufficient evidence. Both proponents and opponents share valid concerns regarding safety and the lack of information on long-term outcomes for vendors. Furthermore, the vast political, cultural, and religious differences between Iran and the United States might make in-depth comparative analyses of little value. But, given that thousands of Americans die each year waiting for a kidney, rejecting the Iranian system out of hand, and without careful analysis, is ill-advised. While the Iranian system may not be as successful as that country's transplant professionals claim, concerns voiced by opponents of kidney vending are typically predicated on opposition to organ vending in general rather than any specific concerns about the Iranian system in particular.

The outcomes for recipients of organs from vendors do not appear to be as good as outcomes for recipients of living donor organs, with at least one report of a 10-year organ survival of 44 percent for recipients of organs from living vendors, compared to a 10-year organ survival of 53 percent for recipients of organs from living donors. When compared with outcomes from living related donors in Iran, however, this difference did not reach statistical significance. Why might outcomes not be as good for recipients of organs from vendors? One explanation can be found by examining the socioeconomic demographics of kidney vendors in Iran. In the available literature on the subject, there is widespread agreement that the majority of vendors are "poor." Although this term is often used imprecisely (sometimes it is undefined, but sometimes it denotes living at or below the poverty level in Iran, which means an income of less than $5 per month), there is little reason to doubt the general truth of the assessment. In the United States, some evidence suggests that low socioeconomic status alone is a predictor for the development of kidney disease. That is not to say that *being poor* somehow *causes* kidney disease, but low socioeconomic status may predict exposure to a host of environmental factors (particularly infections) which can increase the risk of developing kidney disease. If kidney vendors in Iran are disproportionately poor, then as a group they are quite possibly more likely to have subclinical kidney disease at the time of their kidney vending. In addition, they may be malnourished or suffer from other conditions which make them a less than ideal source of kidneys. That might also account for the slightly lower organ survival rate in recipients from impoverished donors.

Organ vending is a remarkably effective means of eliminating a country's organ shortage.

The most contentious disagreements in the literature regarding kidney vending in Iran have to do with the personal, physical, and financial consequences for vendors themselves. This issue is complicated by an absence of routine follow-up. Still, the *hypothesis* that the long-term health of vendors is adversely impacted is plausible, since such a conclusion would logically coincide with the slight trend toward worse long-term outcomes for recipients of transplants from kidney vendors.

Since there is no central repository of outcome data for recipients, donors, or vendors in Iran, the information available to outsiders consists of what is published in the medical literature and anecdotal evidence provided by those who live in or visit Iran. Conceivably, both the reassuring and the worrisome reports on vendor outcomes are true, with each report accurately reporting facts in different geographic areas. Absent a system of routine vendor follow-up, just how to integrate reports and popular accounts remains an open question. While the lack of accurate data justifies concern, it does not justify abandoning the idea of organ vending. The solution is to carefully monitor outcomes and adjust the vending system or, if need be, abandon it should results prove unacceptable. . . .

Lessons to Be Learned from the Iranian System

Taking into consideration the concerns described above, the United States can learn important lessons from Iran. Seven such lessons make clear that organ vending is a remarkably effective means of eliminating a country's organ shortage. The only plausible explanation for Iran's accomplishment of eliminating its waiting list for kidneys is its system of organ procurement from living vendors. Twenty years of experience with organ vending in Iran has demonstrated that a vendor system can exist in harmony with both a living-related-donor program and a flourishing deceased-donor program. Far from restricting access to transplantation to the well-off, access to organs in Iran is possible regardless of the recipient's ability to pay.

In addition, the Iranian system has spared that country the atrocities that accompany gray-market organ trafficking, a practice made possible only because desperate recipients from countries such as the United States have no recourse to a legal market in organs.

Presumably, altruism could, persist and even flourish alongside a kidney market in the United States as it does in Iran. Contrary to critics' assertions, the Iranian model of kidney vending does not preclude either living or deceased donation, as demonstrated by stable rates of biologically related living donation, as well as escalating rates of deceased donation. Deceased donation would and should continue in the United

States as it does in Iran. Some have raised the concern that the introduction of market mechanisms would result in lower rates of procurement from living and deceased donors, a claim unsupported by the evidence. The donor system, whether relying on living or deceased donors, permits individuals who are morally committed to *donating* (not selling) their organs to do so. Recipients with moral objections to receiving an organ purchased from a vendor need not pay for that decision with their lives. Instead, those recipients can request that they only receive an organ from a *donor*; and donors who plan on donating at death can stipulate that their organs may be procured only if they are not subsequently sold. If a vendor market in the United States can be as successful in reducing demand as it has in Iran, the recipient pool for deceased donors would be far smaller than it is today, making the actualization of the moral commitment not to receive an organ from a living vendor less likely to be a fatal decision. . . .

Despite vast cultural and political differences between Iran and the United States, much can be learned from the Iranian system.

Reforms advocated by Iranian proponents of their own system of organ vending overlap with safeguards included in organ market proposals for the United States. Both advocate a registry for vendors and donors, as well as lifelong health care coverage, to more clearly define the short- and long-term consequences of exchanging a kidney; and both reserve the right of transplant professionals to veto a vendor's candidacy based on medical judgment alone.

To ground generalizations about long-term outcomes of donors and vendors in verifiable fact, any organ vending system should track the medical, surgical, psychological, and socioeconomic consequences of both organ donation and organ vending. The most obvious way to do this would be to provide lifelong, comprehensive health insurance to living donors and vendors, perhaps making it a mandatory benefit of any privately arranged organ vending agreement. As [transplant specialists] Arthur Matas and Mark Schnitzler have shown [in the 2004 *American Journal of Transplantation* article "Payment for living Donor Kidneys: A Cost-Effectiveness Analysis."], the cost savings to the government of paying for transplantation instead of dialysis are vast. Thus, it might be both cost-effective and morally salutary to compensate vendors with regular tax-free deposits into personal health savings accounts, which vendors could use to purchase comprehensive insurance coverage from private insurers. . . .

Despite vast cultural and political differences between Iran and the United States, much can be learned from the Iranian system. A review of 20 years of experience with a living organ vendor system in Iran reveals successes, deficiencies, and ambiguities. Each of those aspects is instructive for demonstrating what an organ market can be, as well as what it ought to be. If there is a salient irony in the debate over the moral defensibility of the Iranian system, it is that American critics seem disappointed that the Iranians did not follow our lead. But carrying this reasoning to its conclusion would entail admitting that in so doing, Iran would have also incurred our current shortage of organs, our waiting list mortality, and our consequent moral complicity in sustaining an international market in illegal organ trafficking. If the discussion of kidney markets in this country can progress beyond preconceptions as to what can and cannot work, in Iran or elsewhere, to an examination of the example of Iran based on the evidence, that will be a significant step in the right direction.

10

Government Should Provide Health Insurance as Incentive to Organ Donors

John P. Roberts

John P. Roberts is a professor of surgery at University of California at San Francisco and chief of the Division of Transplantation. He also serves on numerous national committees related to organ transplantation science.

Presently in the United States there is a long list of patients waiting to receive a kidney transplant. And while waiting, these patients often require dialysis treatment, which is covered by Medicare at great expense to taxpayers. If the government would set up a program that offers lifetime medical coverage to living kidney donors, more people might choose to donate. The resulting increase in donated kidneys would lead to a decrease in Medicare expenses. Such a federally funded incentive program would be of great benefit to the American people and is supported by numerous medical organizations as well as the Declaration of Istanbul on Organ Trafficking and Transplant Tourism.

The ASTS [American Society of Transplant Surgeons] would like to see a bill introduced in Congress that would provide lifetime Medicare coverage for living donors. The transplant community would support this provision of insur-

John P. Roberts, "Health Insurance as an Incentive for Living Kidney Donation," American Society of Transplant Surgeons (ASTS), February 6, 2009. Copyright © 2008 by the American Society of Transplant Surgeons. All rights reserved. Reproduced by permission.

ance. In a recent poll of our membership, more than 60% of our members would support provision of health insurance to live donors. The American Society of Transplantation's position paper on living donation clearly supports creation of federally funded insurance programs for donors. The Istanbul document [The Declaration of Istanbul on Organ Trafficking and Transplant Tourism] supports health insurance for donors.

The provision of Medicare will also solve the issue of tracking the outcome of donors in the long term.

More Organ Donation Means Less Cost to Taxpayers

The provision of health insurance removes a major disincentive to donation—the lack of health insurance at the time of donation and in the future. It removes the fear that short- or long-term complications of donation will result in out-of-pocket expenses for the donor. It removes the fear that a donor will not be able to find health care coverage after donation. Up to 15% of organ donors are concerned about insurability and this may affect their willingness to donate.

The provision of Medicare to the donor makes a great deal of financial sense. To the extent that such a program would increase organ donation, it would result in a decrease in the cost of dialysis for patients who are transplant candidates. It has been estimated that each living donor kidney decreases overall healthcare costs by 94,579 in 2002 dollars or about 126,000 in 2009 dollars accounting for medical inflation. With the long waiting time for transplantation and with what appears to be the upper limits on deceased donor transplantation the costs for dialysis versus transplantation are enormous and will continue to grow.

What about the cost of such a program? When we think about patients who are evaluated for donation, each donor undergoes rigorous evaluation of their health. Those who pass the testing are going to be healthy, without diabetes, hypertension, heart disease, or cancer. Because the majority of donors are under age 50, these healthy donors would have low health care costs for many years unless they had a complication of donation, which we would all agree should be covered by some type of insurance. This graph below shows the cost of healthcare for donors until they reach the age of 65 based upon per member per month estimates of health care costs. Therefore at least in the short- and mid-term, the cost savings are going to outweigh the costs.

Since Medicare currently pays for a large portion of the dialysis costs in the United States, having Medicare pick up the costs of the donor's health insurance makes a lot of sense. In a "pay as you go" Congress, it would generate a cost saving that would offset the expense of the donor's healthcare. Even if those who currently had private insurance switched to Medicare, the proven health of these patients would probably result in very low utilization until many of the donors would reach the age of 65.

The Provision of Medicare Offers Many Advantages

The provision of Medicare will also solve the issue of tracking the outcome of donors in the long term. Currently, it is hard for the centers to maintain surveillance of donors after donation because the donors gradually drift away from the center. Current efforts to find the donors 20 years after kidney donation, the time period of concern about long-term renal function, result in finding 1 in 2 donors. With Medicare as the source of health care payments, it becomes easier to follow the outcome of the donors. This will help all donors in the long run.

Without a doubt, in the United States, where 40% of Americans do not have health insurance, the provision of Medicare to organ donors could be a financial incentive. But as incentives go, this provides a lot of advantages. First, it is not a cash payment which was opposed by a majority of our membership. Cash payments have a number of problems associated with them. Health insurance circumvents a number of these issues in that it is a lifetime benefit to the donor, it cannot be traded or sold, and it prevents the disincentives of donation. Will it interfere with those motivated to donate? It is hard to imagine how the provision of health care to the donors would inhibit those who want to donate to their loved one, but it may remove a disincentive to donation. We cannot see how the provision of health insurance would cheapen the act for those motivated to donate to a loved one.

Because Medicare is only available to US citizens, it would not provide an inducement for foreign nationals to come to the United States to donate.

Would it provide incentive to donate to those who do not have an intended recipient? One would hope that it might, given the death rate of patients on the waiting list, the cost of dialysis, and the price that time waiting on the list extracts from survival following kidney transplantation.

Problems with Health Insurance Compensation Would Be Unlikely

Would health insurance be too much inducement, leading to donation by the desperate and economically disadvantaged? This also seems unlikely as the insurance is of little value to anyone other the donor, so it would have no market value. One could imagine that someone who is employed could benefit from not having to enroll in a corporate insurance program and save a few thousand dollars per year, but this is hardly enough for those desperate for the quick buck or the economically disadvantaged. Because Medicare is only available to US citizens, it would not provide an inducement for foreign nationals to come to the United States to donate. There is not a slippery slope awaiting us if we take this step as an incentive for live organ donation.

What are the potential problems with offering long-term health care to donors?

Within the US, offering health insurance may lead to donors coming forward with medical problems that need therapy and that are not disclosed. It seems unlikely that the donor evaluation would miss an otherwise previously diagnosed health problem, but appropriate safeguards would be needed to prevent this from occurring. Those who are ruled out for donation would not receive the health care benefit. A system would need to be set up to evaluate donors who do not have a designated recipient. There would be some expense associated with doing this and there will be questions about whether it should be done within the transplant centers, the organ procurement organizations, or on some other basis.

In sum, the provision of long-term healthcare in the form of Medicare to living donors has a lot to be said for it.

Organizations to Contact

The editors have compiled the following list of organizations concerned with the issues debated in this book. The descriptions are derived from materials provided by the organizations. All have publications or information available for interested readers. The list was compiled on the date of publication of the present volume; names; addresses, phone and fax numbers, and e-mail and Internet addresses may change. Be aware that many organizations take several weeks or longer to respond to inquiries, so allow as much time as possible.

American Society of Transplant Surgeons (ASTS)
2461 South Clark St., Suite 640, Arlington, VA   22202
(703) 414-7870 • fax: (703) 414-7874
website: www.asts.org

The American Society of Transplant Surgeons is comprised of over nearly 1,200 transplant surgeons, physicians, and scientists who are dedicated to education and research in all aspects of organ donation and transplantation. The ASTS seeks to advance the practice of transplantation and to guide those who make policy decisions that influence transplantation. Several of the organization's position statements focus on the ethics of donor compensation, including "Health Insurance as Incentive for Living Kidney Donation" and "Paired Kidney Donation." The society also offers educational videos, which includes "Living Liver Donation: What Are the Risks and Benefits."

American Society of Transplantation (AST)
15000 Commerce Parkway, Suite C, Mt. Laurel, NJ   08054
(856) 439-9986 • fax: (856) 439-9982
e-mail: info@a-s-t.org
website: www.a-s-t.org

Founded in 1982, the American Society of Transplantation is an international organization of transplant professionals aimed at advancing the field of transplantation. Through awareness campaigns and public programs, the AST promotes current transplantation research and patient advocacy methods. The AST regularly publishes research in several publications including the *American Journal of Transplantation* and *Conversations in Transplantation*.

Center for Organ Recovery and Education (CORE)
204 Sigma Dr., RIDC Park, Pittsburgh, PA   15238
(800) 366-6777 • fax: (412) 963-3563
e-mail: sfuller@core.org
website: www.core.org

The Center for Organ Recovery and Education is one of 58 federally designated not-for-profit organ procurement organizations in the United States. The organization is dedicated to promoting donation, education, and research for the purpose of saving and improving the quality of life through organ, tissue, and corneal transplantation. In addition to supporting families during the grieving process and talking with them about the opportunity to donate, the agency also notifies the organ transplant team and coordinates the surgical recovery of organs, tissue, and eyes. CORE also is responsible for facilitating the computerized matching of donated organs and replacement corneas. CORE's website publishes press releases, a "Facts and Statistics" section, as well as various brochures, including *Top 10 Myths about Donation*.

Children's Organ Transplant Association (COTA)
2501 West COTA Dr., Bloomington, IN   47403
(800) 366-2682 • fax: (812) 336-8885
e-mail: cota@cota.org
website: www.cota.org

Founded in 1986, the Children's Organ Transplant Association is a national charity based in Bloomington, Indiana, which is dedicated to organizing and guiding families and communities in raising funds for transplant-needy patients. COTA's priority is to assure that no child or young adult is denied a transplant or excluded from a transplant waiting list due to lack of funds. Among the organization's publications are current press releases and a monthly e-newsletter.

Global Organization for Organ Donation (GOOD)

P.O. Box 52757, Tulsa, OK 74105
(918) 605-1994 • fax: (918) 745-6637
e-mail: info@global-good.org
website: www.global-good.org

The Global Organization for Organ Donation is a nonprofit organization dedicated to saving lives; raising awareness for organ, eye, and tissue donation; correcting misconceptions about donation; and increasing the number of people willing to donate life. GOOD's "Circle of Life" newspaper campaign helps people understand more about the donation process, gives donor and recipient families a way to tell their important stories about donation, and provides newspapers, organ procurement organizations, and funeral homes the information they need to become participating partners. In addition, GOOD issues press releases about facts and myths regarding the ethics of organ donation, including compensation for organs.

HumanTrafficking.org

1825 Connecticut Ave. NW, Washington, DC 20009-5721
(202) 884-8000 • fax: (202) 884-8405
e-mail: bertone.andrea@gmail.com
website: www.humantrafficking.org

The purpose of HumanTrafficking.org is to bring government and non-government organizations in East Asia and the Pacific together to cooperate and learn from each other's experiences in efforts to combat human trafficking. The site contains country-specific information, such as national laws and action plans, and descriptions of various organizations' activities worldwide. In addition to its monthly newsletter and a library of publications on human trafficking in general, a special section of the website focuses on the trafficking of human organs.

National Human Genome Research Institute (NHGRI)

National Institutes of Health, Building 31, Room 4B09
31 Center Drive, MSC 2152, 9000 Rockville Pike
Bethesda, MD   20892
(301) 402-0911 • fax: (301) 402-2218
website: www.genome.gov

The National Human Genome Research Institute, originally the National Center for Human Genome Research, was re-named in 1997 by the US Department of Health and Human Services, which officially elevated it to the status of research institute—one of twenty-seven institutes and centers that make up the National Institutes of Health. The NHGRI supports the development of resources and technology that will accelerate genome research and its application to human health. A critical part of the NHGRI mission is the study of the ethical, legal, and social implications of genome research. NHGRI also supports the training of investigators and the dissemination of genome information to the public and to health professionals. Among the institute's many publications are current news releases, recent articles, speeches, and testimony, and fact sheets about science, ethics, and research technique, including *The Ethical, Legal and Social Implications Research Program* and *Genetic Information Nondiscrimination Act of 2008.*

National Kidney Foundation (NKF)

30 East 33rd St., New York, NY   10016
(800) 622-9010 • fax: (212) 689-9261
website: www.kidney.org

The National Kidney Foundation, a major voluntary nonprofit health organization, is dedicated to preventing kidney and urinary tract diseases, improving the health and well-being of individuals and families affected by kidney disease, and increasing the availability of all organs for transplantation. NKF raises awareness about kidney health and the importance of early detection through the national "Love Your Kidneys" public service campaign, news releases, free brochures, and local education programs. NKF offers various publications, including the *Family Focus Newsletter, Love Your Kidneys Newsletter,* the quarterly newsletter *Transplant Chronicles,* and the *Capital Kidney Connection,* which highlights legislative and regulatory initiatives.

OrganSelling.com

(412) 648-9443
e-mail: htk@pitt.edu
website: www.organselling.com

OrganSelling.com is a website devoted to collecting information about establishing a worldwide free market organ trade in which donors would be compensated for their organs. In addition to a statement of purpose, the site also offers links to the most recent research done on donor compensation, a patient stories section, and a forum for visitors to discuss organ transplantation issues.

Transplant Recipients International Organization (TRIO)

2100 M St. NW, #170-353, Washington, DC   20037
(202) 293-0980
e-mail: info@trioweb.org
website: www.trioweb.org

The Transplant Recipients International Organization a nonprofit international organization committed to improving the quality of lives touched by transplantation through support, advocacy, education, and awareness. One of its major efforts involves taking the concerns and needs that affect the welfare of transplant candidates, recipients, and their families to federal, state, and local government bodies. In addition to regularly publishing the *Lifelines* newsletter, TRIO also posts position statements about organ donation, including "Your Choice First! A Presumed Consent Policy for Organ Donation" and "The Trouble with: 1—Paying Cash for Organs; 2—Presumed Consent; 3—Putting Signed-up Donors at the Head of the List."

United Network for Organ Sharing (UNOS)
P.O. Box 2484, Richmond, VA   23218
(888) 894-6361
website: www.unos.org

Located in Richmond, Virginia, the United Network for Organ Sharing is a nonprofit, scientific and educational organization that administers the nation's Organ Procurement and Transplantation Network, established by the US Congress in 1984. UNOS's mission is to advance organ availability and transplantation by uniting and supporting communities for the benefit of patients through education, technology, and policy development. In addition to fact sheets and patient brochures, UNOS offers *E-News* for the latest organ transplantation and donation news.

World Health Organization (WHO)
Avenue Appia 20, 1211 Geneva 27, Switzerland
41-22-791-21-11 • fax: 41-22-791-31-11
e-mail: info@who.int
website: www.who.int

The World Health Organization is the directing and coordinating authority for health within the United Nations system. It is responsible for providing leadership on global health matters, shaping the health research agenda, setting norms and standards, articulating evidence-based policy options, providing technical support to countries, and monitoring and assessing health trends. Among the organization's publications are the monthly *Bulletin* and the annual *World Health Report*, and several of its many investigative reports have focused on the buying and selling human organs.

Bibliography

Books

Rene Almeling — *Sex Cells: The Medical Market for Eggs and Sperm*. Berkeley, CA: University of California Press, 2011.

Katrina A. Bramstedt and Rena Down — *The Organ Donor Experience: Good Samaritans and the Meaning of Altruism*. Lanham, MD: Rowman & Littlefield, 2011.

Naomi R. Cahn — *Test Tube Families: Why the Fertility Market Needs Legal Regulation*. New York: New York University Press, 2009.

Annie Cheney — *Body Brokers: Inside America's Underground Trade in Human Remains*. New York: Broadway Books, 2006.

Mark J. Cherry — *Kidney for Sale by Owner: Human Organs, Transplantation, and the Market*. Washington, DC: Georgetown University Press, 2005.

Melinda Cooper — *Life as Surplus: Biotechnology and Capitalism in the Neoliberal Era*. Seattle, WA: University of Washington Press, 2008.

Michele Goodwin — *Black Markets: The Supply and Demand of Body Parts*. New York: Cambridge University Press, 2006.

Kieran Joseph Healy — *Last Best Gifts: Altruism and the Market for Human Blood and Organs.* Chicago: University of Chicago Press, 2006.

David Koepsell — *Who Owns You?: The Corporate Gold-Rush to Patent Your Genes.* Malden, MA: Wiley-Blackwell, 2009.

Susan E. Lederer — *Flesh and Blood: Organ Transplantation and Blood Transfusion in Twentieth-Century America.* New York: Oxford University Press, 2008.

David Matas and David Kilgour — *Bloody Harvest: Organ Harvesting of Falun Gong Practitioners in China.* Woodstock, Ontario, Canada: Seraphim Editions, 2009.

Lisa Jean Moore — *Sperm Counts: Overcome by Man's Most Precious Fluid.* New York: New York University Press, 2007.

Liza Mundy — *Everything Conceivable: How Assisted Reproduction Is Changing Men, Women, and the World.* New York: Alfred A. Knopf, 2007.

David Plotz — *The Genius Factory: The Curious History of the Nobel Prize Sperm Bank.* New York: Random House, 2005.

Nikolas Rose — *The Politics of Life Itself: Biomedicine, Power, and Subjectivity in the Twenty-First Century.* Princeton, NJ: Princeton University Press, 2007.

Lesley Alexandra Sharp	*Strange Harvest: Organ Transplants, Denatured Bodies, and the Transformed Self.* Berkeley, CA: University of California Press, 2006.
Debora L. Spar	*The Baby Business: How Money, Science, and Politics Drive the Commerce of Conception.* Boston: Harvard Business School Press, 2006.
Catherine Waldby and Robert Mitchell	*Tissue Economies: Blood, Organs, and Cell Lines in Late Capitalism.* Durham, NC: Duke University Press, 2006.

Periodicals and Internet Sources

JoNel Aleccia	"Killer's Quest: Allow Organ Donation After Execution," MSNBC.com, April 21, 2011.
Rene Almeling	"Gender and the Value of Bodily Goods: Commodification in Egg and Sperm Donation," *Law and Contemporary Problems*, Summer 2009.
Ronald Bailey	"Fresh Kidneys for Sale: International Organ Markets Aren't the Same as Slave Markets," *Reason.com*, October 13, 2009. www.reason.com.
Naomi R. Cahn	"Making Laws about Making Babies: End the Anonymity," *New York Times*, September 13, 2011.

Alastair V. Campbell | "No Such Thing as Ethical Organ Market," Asiaone, July 11, 2008. www.asiaone.com.

Scott Carney | "Foreign Policy: Strict Laws Perpetuate Organ Theft," NPR, June 6, 2011. www.npr.org.

So Yeon Choe | "Exploring Alternatives to Organ Commodification," *Yale Journal of Medicine and Law*, Vol. VII, No. 1, October 5, 2010.

Abdallah S. Daar | "The Case for a Regulated System of Living Kidney Sales," *Nature*, Vol. 2, No. 11, November 2006.

Marcy Darnovsky and Jesse Reynolds | "The Battle to Patent Your Genes: The Meaning of the Myriad Case," *American Interest*, September–October 2009.

Tony Dokoupil | "You Got Your Sperm Where?" *Newsweek*, October 2, 2011.

Paul Elias | "Most Bone Marrow Donors Can Be Paid, Court Rules," Associated Press, December 2, 2011.

D.S. Epperson | "Plasma Donations Put a Price on Human Life," EzineArticles.com, June 11, 2009. http://ezinearticles.com.

Cory Franklin | "Myth or Fact? Human Organ Trafficking," *Chicago Life Magazine*, December 14, 2010.

Diana Furchtgott-Roth | "New Hope on Organ Donation," *New York Sun*, September 24, 2008.

Harold Gershowitz and Amy Gershowitz Lask — "Our Deeply Unethical National Organ Policy," *American*, July 7, 2010.

Michael Gormley — "New York to Be First Organ Donor Opt-Out State?" *Huffington Post*, April 27, 2010. www.huffingtonpost.com.

Leo Hickman — "The Cost of Body Parts Around the World," *Guardian*, July 27, 2009.

Kerry Howley — "Who Owns Your Body Parts? Everyone's Making Money in the Market for Body Tissue—Except the Donors," *Reason*, March 2007.

Jeneen Interlandi — "Not Just Urban Legend," *Daily Beast*, January 9, 2009.

Christian Longo — "Giving Life After Death Row," *New York Times*, March 5, 2011.

Vijay K. Mathur — "Remedying Organ Transplant Shortage Requires Financial Incentives," *Standard Examiner*, July 2, 2011.

Robyn Nazar — "The Value of an Egg Donation," *American Fertility Association*, July 30, 2011.

Jessica Pauline Ogilvie — "The Consequenses of a Donor Kidney Market," *Los Angeles Times*, March 28, 2011.

Rachel Rettner   "Great Debate: Should Organ Donors Be Paid?" *Live Science*, August 10, 2009.

William Saletan   "The Egg Market," *Slate.com*, March 29, 2010. www.slate.com.

Sandy Sand   "Selling Body Parts to Make Ends Meet a Sign of the Times," *Digital Journal*, February 25, 2009. http://digitaljournal.com.

Angie Sandoval   "Mexicans Cross US Border to Sell Their Plasma," MSNBC, November 23, 2011. www.msnbc.com.

Sally Satel   "Yuan a Kidney?: China's Proposals to Pay Organ Donors Flout the Status Quo. That's a Good Thing." *Slate.com*, June 13, 2011. www.slate.com.

Nancy   "The Organ Donors' Bill of Rights,"
Scheper-Hughes   *New Internationalist Magazine*, September 22, 2010.

John Schwartz   "Judge Invalidates Human Gene
and Andrew   Patent," *New York Times*, March 29,
Pollack   2010.

Michael Smith   "Kidneys at Hub of Deadly 'Transplant Tourism,'" *News Tribune*, May 15, 2011.

Claire Suddath   "How Does Kidney Trafficking
and Alex Altman   Work?" *Time*, July 27, 2009.

Jeff Whitehead   "The Harvest: Human Organs and
                      Human Security," *Human Security
                      Journal*, Vol. 6, Spring 2008.

James Wilsterman   "The Human Commodity," *Harvard
                      Crimson*, June 4, 2008.

Jennifer Wolff   "Your Eggs: Buy Sell Freeze?"
                      Women's Health, January–February
                      2011.

Index